OAKWOOD LIBRARY OF RAILWAY HISTORY OL 163

Sunderland's Railways

Neil T. Sinclair

Electric locomotive built in 1901 by British Thompson Houston for Sunderland Corporation's electricity generating station crossing the tram lines and wires at Hylton Road in 1952 on the short line from the exchange sidings beside the coal depot served by Hetton Colliery Railway.

THE OAKWOOD PRESS

© 2019 Neil T. Sinclair

First edition published by Tyne and Wear Museum Service
as Railways of Sunderland 1985
Second edition 1986

This edition published in the United Kingdom, 2019
The Oakwood Press
54-58 Mill Square, Catrine, KA5 6RD
www.stenlake.co.uk

Printed by
P2D Books, 1 Newlands Rd, Westoning, Bedford, MK45 5LD

ISBN 978-0-85361-462-3

In memory of Ian S. Carr, Sunderland Railway Photographer

Front cover: NCB 0-6-2T No. 52 (Neilson Reid, 1899) on the Hetton Colliery Railway crosses over the Penshaw branch north of Chester Road in 1957 with the spire of St Peter's Presbyterian Church in the left background. The locomotive is conveying loaded wagons away from the direction of the staiths for the Chester Road Landsale as this only had a facing connection for trains coming from Hetton.

Back cover: 'J27' class 0-6-0 No. 65854 with a coal train from Hylton Colliery has stalled on the steep gradient at Southwick in 1963. It was necessary to divide the train. On the right are wagons which have carried steel plate to Austin and Pickersgill's shipyard.

Contents

Picture Credits and Further Reading 4
Preface and Acknowledgments 5
The Development of Sunderland's Railways
    Wagonways to the Wear 9
    The Colliery Railways and the First Public Railways 1812 – 1840 14
    The Hudson Era and the Docks 1841 – 1855 20
    The North Eastern Railway 1855 – 1899 24
    The North Eastern and the Colliery Railways 1900 – 1922 27
    The LNER 1923 – 1947 32
    British Railways and the National Coal Board 1948 – 1994 35
    A Passenger Railway 1995 – 2018 40
The Railway Staff 45
Sunderland Railway Lines
    The Lambton Railway 53
    The Hetton Colliery Railway 61
    The Lambton and Hetton Staiths 67
    The Brandling Junction Railway 71
    The Monkwearmouth Junction Railway 79
    The Durham and Sunderland and Londonderry Railways 87
    The South Docks 99
    The Old Main Line 104
    The Stanhope and Tyne and Hylton, Southwick and
    Monkwearmouth Railways. 108
    The Penshaw Branch 113

Illustration Credits

J.W. Armstrong (Armstrong Railway Photographic Trust): pages 86 (lwr), 87

Author: 21 (upr), 41 (lwr), 43, 60 (lwr), 74 (lwr), 78 (both), 83 (upr), 84 (both), 110 (lwr), 111 (lwr), 112 (both), 118 (lwr), 122 (lwr), 123 (lwr)

J.M. Boyes (Armstrong Railway Photographic Trust): 114 (lwr)

W.A. Camwell (Armstrong Railway Photographic Trust): 33

Ian S. Carr (Armstrong Railway Photographic Trust): Front and back covers, 10 (lwr), 34 (lwr), 35, 36, 37 (both), 38, 39, 41 (upr), 51, 54, 55 (upr), 56 (both), 57 (both), 58 (both), 59 (lwr), 61, 62, 63 (both), 64 (lwr), 65 (both), 68 (upr), 70 (both), 72 (lwr), 73, 75 (upr), 76 (upr), 79 (upr), 80 (lwr), 81 (lwr), 82, 83 (lwr), 85 (both), 89, 91 (upr), 92 (lwr), 93 (both), 94 (both), 95 (both), 96 (lwr), 98 (lwr), 100 (upr), 101 (both), 102 (both), 104, 105 (both), 106 (both), 107 (both), 108, 109 (both), 110 (upr), 111 (upr), 113, 114 (upr), 115 (lwr), 115 (lwr), 116 (lwr), 117 (both), 118 (upr), 119 (both), 120 (lwr), 121 (lwr), 122 (upr), 123 (upr), 124 (both)

G. Edwards: 98 (upr)

P. Gray: 50 (left)

M. Grimes: 42, 77 (lwr), 92 (upr), 96 (upr), 97 (both), 103 (lwr), 115 (upr)

Sunderland Antiquarian Society: 16

Sunderland Echo 1, 2, 80 (upr)

Sunderland Museum and Winter Gardens: 11 (both), 12, 13, 14, 15 (both), 17, 18 (lwr),19, 20, 21, 24, 25, 26, 27, 28 (lwr), 29, 30, 31, 32, 34, 44 (lwr), 46, 47 (both). 48 (both), 49 (upr), 53, 59 (upr), 67, 68 (lwr), 69 (upr), 72 (upr), 76 (upr), 77 (upr), 79 (lwr), 81 (upr), 90 (both), 91 (lwr), 100 (lwr), 103 (upr), 116 (upr), 120 (upr), 121 (upr)

S.E. Teasdale (Author's Collection): 71 (both)

J Temple: 50 (right)

C.H. Townley: 87 (upr)

V. Wake: (Armstrong Railway Photographic Trust: 88

N. Whaler: 44 (upr), 49 (lwr), 75 (lwr)

The remainder of the illustrations are from the author's collection

Further Reading

J. Addyman and B, Fawcett, *Thomas Elliot Harrison* (Rocket Press, 2008).

R. Beaumont, *The Railway King* (Review, 2002).

S. Bragg, *North Eastern Railway 1:5000 Atlas 1922* (Industrialogical Associates, 2005).

I.S. Carr, *Railscenes Around Sunderland* (Tyne and Wear Museums, 1988).

R. R. Darsley, *Darlington – Leamside – Newcastle* (Middleton Press, 2008).

B. Fawcett, *A History of North Eastern Railway Architecture Volumes 1, 2, 3* (North Eastern Railway Association, 2001, 2003, 2005).

A. Guy, *Steam and Speed: Railways of Tyne and Wear from the Earliest Days* (Tyne Bridge Publishing, 2003).

K. Hoole, *North Eastern Locomotive Sheds* (David & Charles, 1972).

K. Hoole, *The Regional History of the Railways of Great Britain: North East England* (David & Charles, 1974).

K. Hoole, *Railways Stations of the North East* (David & Charles, 1985).

R. J. Irving, *The North Eastern Railway Company 1870 -1914: An Economic History* (Leicester University Press, 1976).

R. Langham, *The North Eastern Railway in the First World War* (Fonthill Media, 2013).

C.E. Mountford, *The Private Railways of County Durham* (Industrial Railway Society, 2004).

C.E. Mountford, *The Industrial Railways & Locomotives of County Durham Volumes 1 & 2* (Industrial Railway Society, 2006, 2009).

C.E. Mountford, *Rope & Chain Haulage* (Industrial Railway Society, 2013).

M. Quick, *Railway Passenger Stations in Great Britain* (Railway & Canal Historical Society, 2009).

N.T. Sinclair, 'Industry to 1914' in G.E. Milburn and S.T. Miller (Editors), S*underland, River Town and People* (Thomas Reed, 1988).

N.T. Sinclair, *Sunderland City and People Since 1945* (Breedon Books, 2004).

W.W. Tomlinson, *The North Eastern Railway: Its Rise and Development* (Reprint by David & Charles, 1967 of 1914 original).

C. von Oeynhausen and H. von Dechen, *Railways in England 1826 and 1827* (Newcomen Society, 1971).

C.R. Warn, *Rails Between Wear and Tyne* (Frank Graham, 1982).

In addition to the books published above, the North Eastern Railway Association also produces a quarterly magazine, *The North Eastern Express*, with historical articles about the region's railways. Further details of the Association can be found at www.ner.org.uk

Preface and Acknowledgements

This book is an illustrated survey of the railways that existed within present day boundaries of the City of Sunderland. It concentrates on the lines that became part of the North Eastern Railway and the Lambton and Hetton Colliery railways, but also covers several of the other colliery and industrial wagonways and railways in the area. The railways covered include short sections which leave the City boundaries and then re-enter them.

When the first wagonways were built to the Wear, Sunderland was the name given to the township on the south bank of the Wear at the mouth of the river. The name covered a wider area after the Borough of Sunderland was created in 1835, as this also included the townships of Bishopwearmouth and Monkwearmouth. Over the next century municipal boundaries were expanded to take in the surrounding villages, such as Pallion, Southwick and Fulwell which had become physically linked to the growing town. In 1967 and then in 1974 a wider area, including Ryhope, South Hylton, Washington, Houghton and Hetton, became part of the local authority, which was created a city in 1992. In the main text of this book the term Sunderland is used for the boundaries before 1967.

Sunderland's Railways is a successor to my *Railways of Sunderland*, two editions of which were published by Tyne and Wear Museums Service in 1985 and 1986. This book details the significant changes that have taken place since 1986, including the end of coal traffic from Wearside and the extension of the Tyne and Wear Metro to the City. The sections on wagonways and early railways also incorporate recent research, particularly that by Colin E. Mountford whose books are listed under Further Reading.

The *Railways of Sunderland* book owed much to my friend Ian S. Carr who provided almost half the illustrations and provided much help with the text. Several years ago, Ian and I discussed producing a new book on the City's railways, but his ill health in the years leading up to his death in 2015 prevented this. The present book again owes much to Ian's photographs, which are now held by the Armstrong Railway Photographic Trust. It is dedicated to the memory of this outstanding photographer who recorded the railways of his home town for over 50 years.

For providing illustrations I am grateful to the Armstrong Railway Photographic Trust, Sunderland Museum and Winter Gardens and all those listed in the acknowledgements on page four. I would also like to thank Mark Grimes, Colin Mountford, Martin Routledge, Ashley Sutherland, Alan Thompson and Neville Whaler for their help with this book

Neil T. Sinclair

Railways about 1840

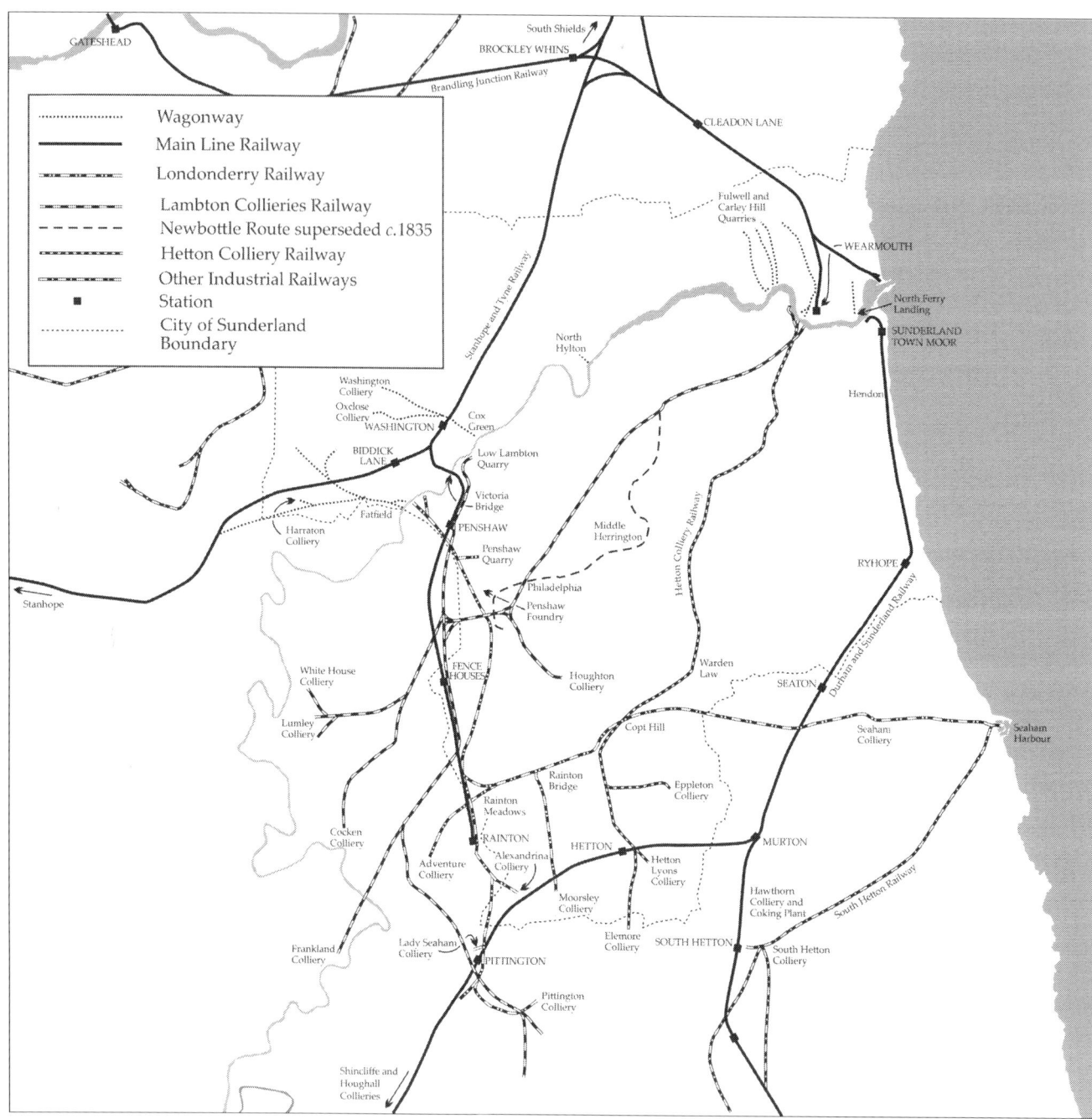

Railways from 1915 to 1965
including lines and stations opened and closed during those years

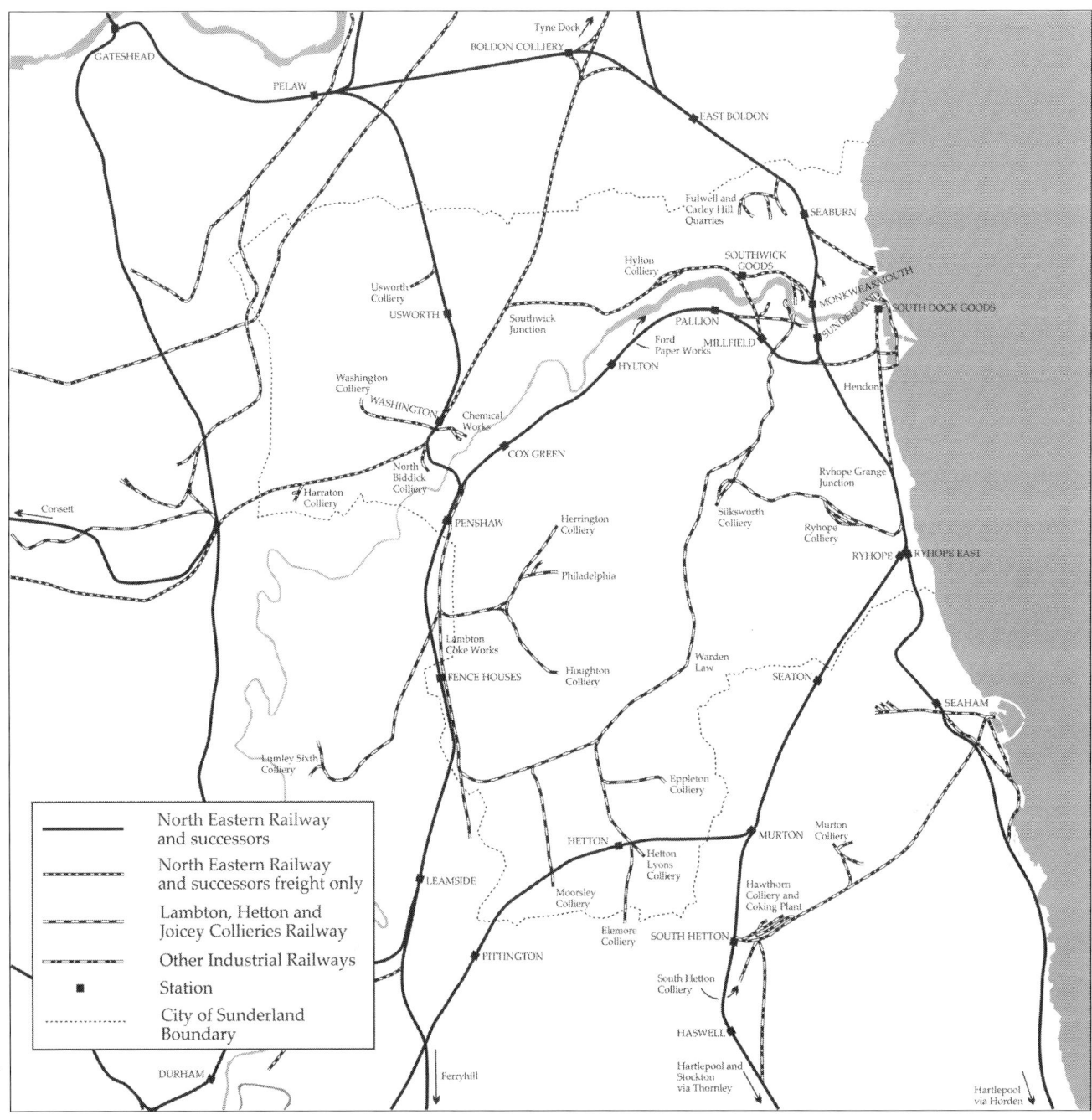

Railways that have existed within the boundaries of the original Borough of Sunderland, Southwick and Fulwell

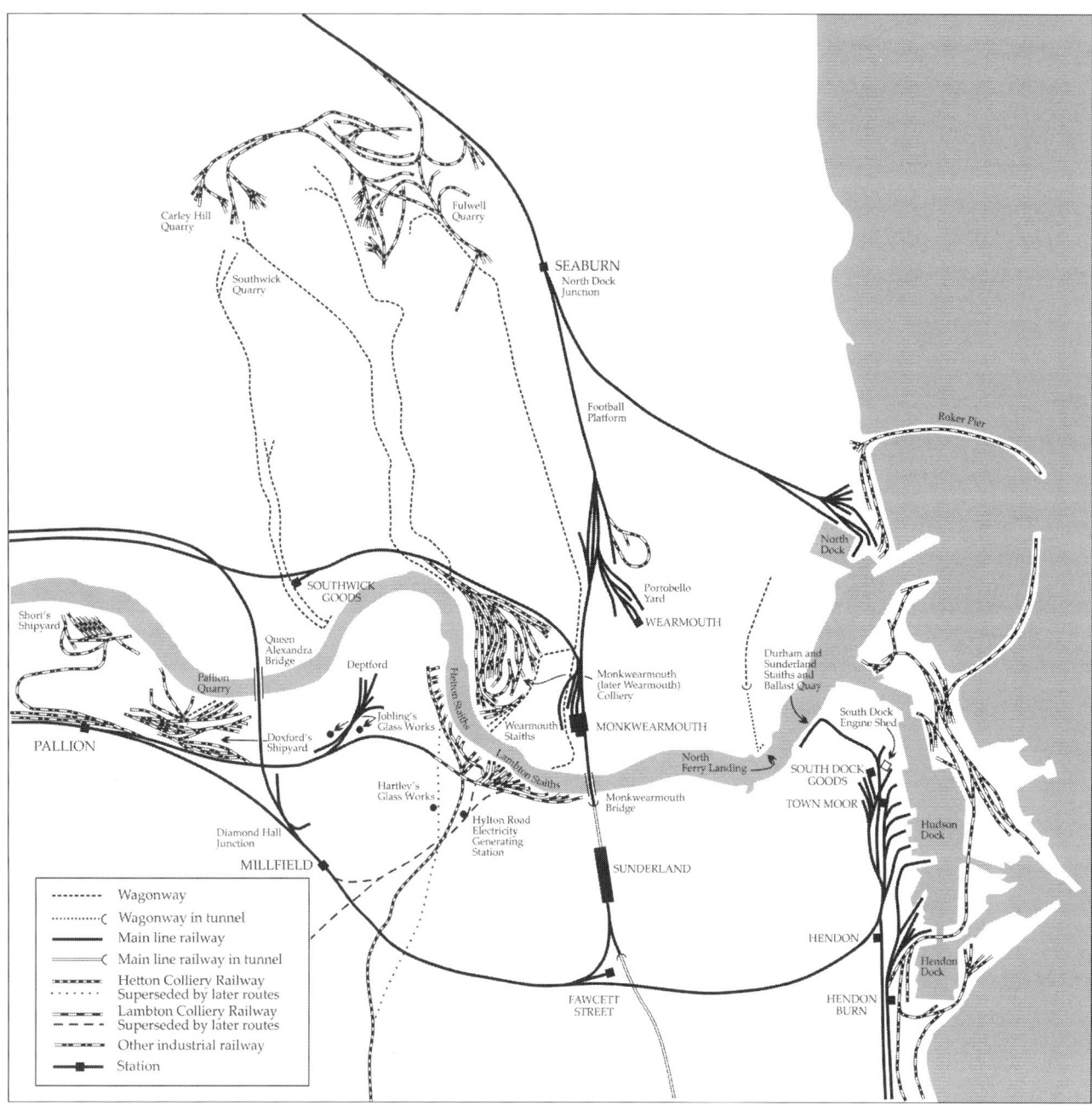

The Development of Sunderland's Railways

Wagonways to the Wear

The main factors which stimulated the early development of railways on Wearside were the coal pits and limestone quarries in the area along with the River Wear. This provided a link to the North Sea and to markets for these minerals on the East Coast of Britain.

Transport of coal from pits to staiths at the nearest navigable point on the Wear was the reason why the first wagonways were built. Wearside's geology meant that until the 19th century all collieries were concentrated west of Herrington. East of Herrington the coal measures were thought not to exist as they were concealed by the Permian Magnesian Limestone and Yellow Sand. So, the earliest railways in the town of Sunderland were wagonways which took limestone to kilns on the river banks.

Colliery wagonways in the Fatfield and Cox Green districts, initially with wooden rails, were built from the 17th century. Burleigh and Thompson's map of 1737 shows 17 staiths or spouts. Coal was loaded into keels (coal-carrying barges) and taken to Sunderland where it was transferred again, this time into sea-going collier ships.

In the early 19th century John Buddle (1772-1843) the country's leading colliery engineer devised a system of loading coal into tubs at the collieries which were then moved onto specially built keels. At Sunderland the tubs were tipped into the colliers by a crane. A steam-powered crane was built for this purpose immediately west of the iron bridge at Monkwearmouth.

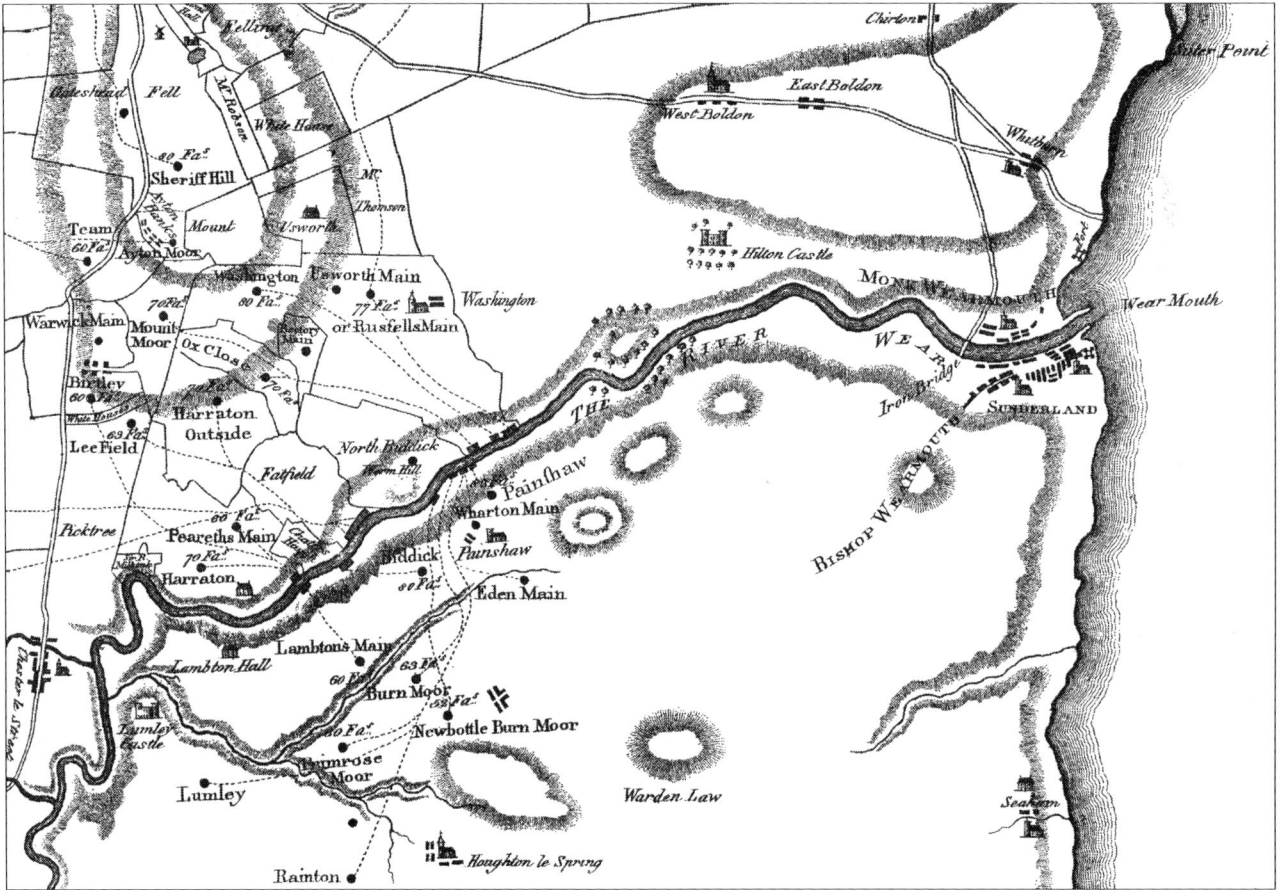

Section of William Cason's map of 1801 which shows the wagonways leading to the staiths on the Wear between Chartershaugh (north bank, near Harraton House) and Cox Green (unmarked, near Painshaw on the south bank).

Detail from print after J.W. Carmichael's painting of the Victoria Bridge in 1838 showing coal transport on the River Wear. On the left are two keels; that nearer the bank is carrying tubs to be loaded at one of the riverside collieries. On the right are Low Lambton Staiths which continued in use until the end of the 19th century to load stone from Penshaw Quarries and coal for riverside industries not served by railways.

Wooden wagonway rails, of about 4 feet 3 inch gauge, of the Lambton Wagonway which were uncovered during the clearance of the coke works at Fencehouses in 1996. They are believed to date from 1812 to 1817.

The major colliery wagonways to the River Wear, from Fatfield, 8 miles upstream from Sunderland were replaced at the beginning of the 19th century by longer railways. These ran directly to the ports at Sunderland for the Lambton Collieries and at Seaham for the Londonderry Collieries. Coal could now be loaded directly into sea-going ships. Some of the colliery wagonways and keels remained in use until the late 19th century, principally to serve industries on the river banks which did not have railway connections.

A later short colliery line to the staiths on the Wear was that from Pemberton Main (later Monkwearmouth and then Wearmouth) Colliery, opened in 1835 (*see map page 8*). It had taken nine years to sink the shaft through the Permian Limestone. The pit was situated close to the river mouth and sea-going colliers could be loaded directly from the staiths on the Wear reached by an incline. Even though the Brandling Junction Railway reached Monkwearmouth in 1839, the colliery was not linked to the main line railway system until 1876.

Sandstone for building was quarried at Penshaw and transported by river through the Low Lambton Staiths. There was also a wagonway from the sandstone quarry at North Hylton (*see map page 6*). After the North Hylton Quarry closed about 1880 the wagonway was converted to standard gauge and extended uphill to Wood House Farm, from where it was

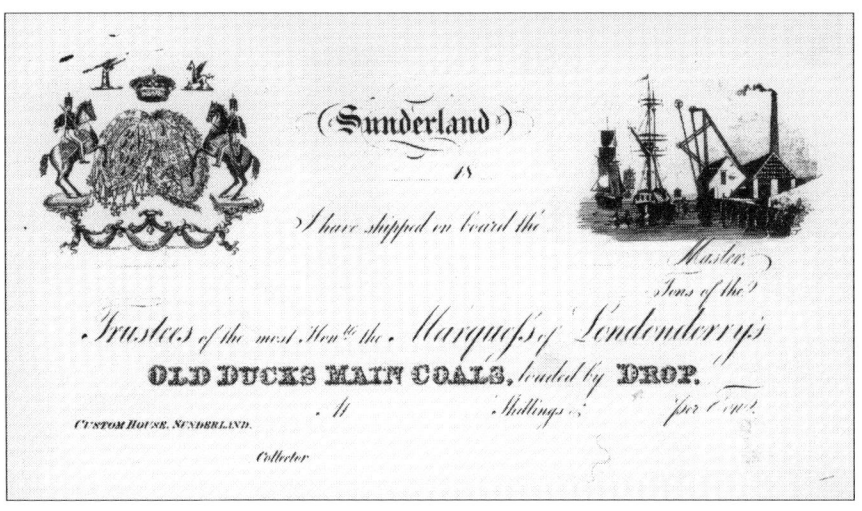

One of the Marquis of Londonderry's coal tickets showing the stationary engine beside Wearmouth Bridge unloading a coal tub into a sea-going ship.

Print of 1850 showing the Southwick Bottle Company's Works. There are several coal carrying keels in the river, as well as larger vessels. A keel with coal is at the bottom of the short incline to the Bottle Works. The chaldron wagon which took the coal to the furnaces, is at the top of the incline.

Etching by E. Swinburne published in 1839 which shows the Carley Hill lime kilns and wagonways. The kiln on the left was served by the wagonway from the Carley Hill West Quarry and that on the right by the wagonway from the East Quarry. Both kilns were reached by inclines operated by horse-powered windlasses. A chaldron wagon with coal from a keel is being drawn up the track running through the centre of the kiln. Workmen on the top of the kiln are feeding in the coal and limestone. The stone sleepers of the Carley Hill West wagonway could be seen in the wide back lane between James Armitage and Edward Burdis Streets until the mid-1970s. The kilns survive today, one of the few reminders of Sunderland's industrial past.

worked by a stationary steam engine. It seems likely that this extended line took manure, including the contents of Sunderland's ash privies, up to the farm for spreading on the fields.

There were several limestone wagonways from quarries in the Pallion, Southwick, Fulwell and Carley Hill areas which were built from the end of the 18th centuries (*see map page 8*). Sunderland was the only port on the North-East coast where limestone was exposed. The wagonways brought limestone to kilns from where the burnt lime was loaded into ships. It was used as an agricultural fertiliser, in building and in industries such as glassmaking and later also in steelmaking.

The short wagonway from the large quarry at Pallion to the adjacent limekilns, which was worked by a stationary engine, only lasted until the quarry closed in the 1830s.

The first line from a quarry at Southwick was replaced when a larger quarry was opened. The wagonway from the second quarry, which led to limekilns operated by Thomas Brunton, was abandoned in the 1840s.

The Fulwell line was built by Sir Hedworth Williamson (1751-1810), from his quarries alongside Newcastle Road to kilns at Sheepfolds, west of the iron bridge, most probably in the 1790s. Its route was diverted to the west when Monkwearmouth station was built in 1848. A spur was built into Wearmouth Colliery which could provide coal for the lime kilns. The Fulwell wagonway was abandoned in the 1870s after the quarry was linked to the North Eastern Railway.

The longest lasting limestone wagonways were those from Carley Hill East and Carley Hill West. The last survivor, the East Wagonway, by now owned by the Wearmouth Coal Company, closed in 1902. The Carley Hill quarries passed to Sir Hedworth Williamson's Limeworks and were linked to the Fulwell quarry railway system. The Carley Hill routes are preserved in the road patterns of the area.

There was a further short wagonway linked to river transport at the North Ferry Landing in Monkwearmouth from the 1800s to the 1860s (*see map page 8*). This took ballast (small stones, chalk and sand) from ships which had arrived without cargo and were about to take coal or lime from the port. The North Ferry Landing was one of several ballast quays near the mouth of the Wear. The ballast wharf on the Low Quay, on the south bank, was linked to the Durham & Sunderland Railway from about 1841 to 1850

The wagonways were predominantly worked by horses, supplemented sometimes by manpower. Haulage on inclines was provided by horse powered windlasses or stationary steam engine, with self-acting inclines on some colliery wagonways.

The ballast wagonway beside the Monkwearmouth North Ferry Landing about 1873. The wagonway ran in a small tunnel from the quay to the area east of St Peter's Church where ballast appears to have been tipped into a second, larger, narrow gauge line terminating to the west of Brandling Street.

The Colliery Railways and the First Public Railways 1812 – 1840

A significant development, which changed the course of the development of railway transport on Wearside, came with the opening of the 4 feet 0 inch gauge Newbottle Railway, engineered by Edward Steel, in 1812 (*see map page 6*). Coal could now be transported directly from the pits to sea-going ships at Sunderland. It was built by the Nesham family from their pits in the Philadelphia area, near Houghton-le-Spring to staiths on the banks of the Wear above the iron bridge in Sunderland. This area was to be a major centre of coal transport from the town for the next 150 years.

The construction of the Newbottle line was initially worked by horses with a self-acting incline to the staiths at Sunderland. By 1818, however, rope haulage had been introduced on other sections with a major reduction in operating costs.

The importance of the Newbottle Railway was clear to the keelmen who saw their livelihood disappear and in March 1815 caused damage costing £6,000 to the Sunderland end of the line. The cavalry were called to quell the riot and the damage was repaired

A steam locomotive built at the Butterley Iron Works in Derbyshire was tried out in 1815 but exploded. An alternative method of dealing with the increasing coal traffic from the Nesham's pits was found by 1818 when rope haulage, powered by stationary steam engines, was introduced on certain sections.

By 1822 John Nesham was in financial difficulties and the Newbottle Wagonway was sold at auction by his trustees. It was bought by John George Lambton (1792-1840 later the 1st Earl of Durham). He linked the railway to his existing 4 feet 2 inch/4 feet 3 inch wagonways in the Penshaw area, thus creating the Lambton Railway system. Two-thirds of the original route of the Newbottle line was abandoned about 1835 and replaced by a more direct line, also rope-worked.

The Hetton Colliery Railway, opened in 1822, linked the newly-sunk pit at Hetton Lyons to staiths at Sunderland, ascending and descending the 636ft of Warden Law along the way (*see map page 6*). This was the beginning

One of several lithographs produced after the Hetton Colliery Railway opened in 1822 when the line was considered a major technological development. At the bottom is a representation of one of George Stephenson's locomotives. The view exaggerates the height of the countryside between Hetton and Sunderland but shows the main features of the line when first opened. It started at the Lyons Colliery (*far right*) and, after locomotive haulage to Hetton Dene, the trucks were hauled by stationary engines at Copt Hill and Warden Law. The wagons then descended using four self-acting inclines to North Moor where locomotives pulled them past the prominent High Barnes House, the home of the Ettrick family, to a self-acting incline to the staiths close to the 1796 cast-iron bridge.

The Development of Sunderland's Railways: The Colliery Railways and the First Public Railways 1812 – 1840

A horse-drawn chaldron wagon as illustrated on a plan of the Newbottle 'Waggon rail way' which was produced in 1817. Another illustration on the map, which showed the route of the railway, was of the iron bridge at Sunderland.

Document containing the names of prominent men who subscribed to a reward for the apprehension of the ringleaders of the keelmen and casters (who transferred coal from the keels to the colliers), whom the *Newcastle Weekly Chronicle* of 25th March, 1815 said had five days earlier, pulled down the bridge carrying the Newbottle Railway across Galley's Gill and set fire to the adjacent coal depot and the self-acting incline to the staiths.

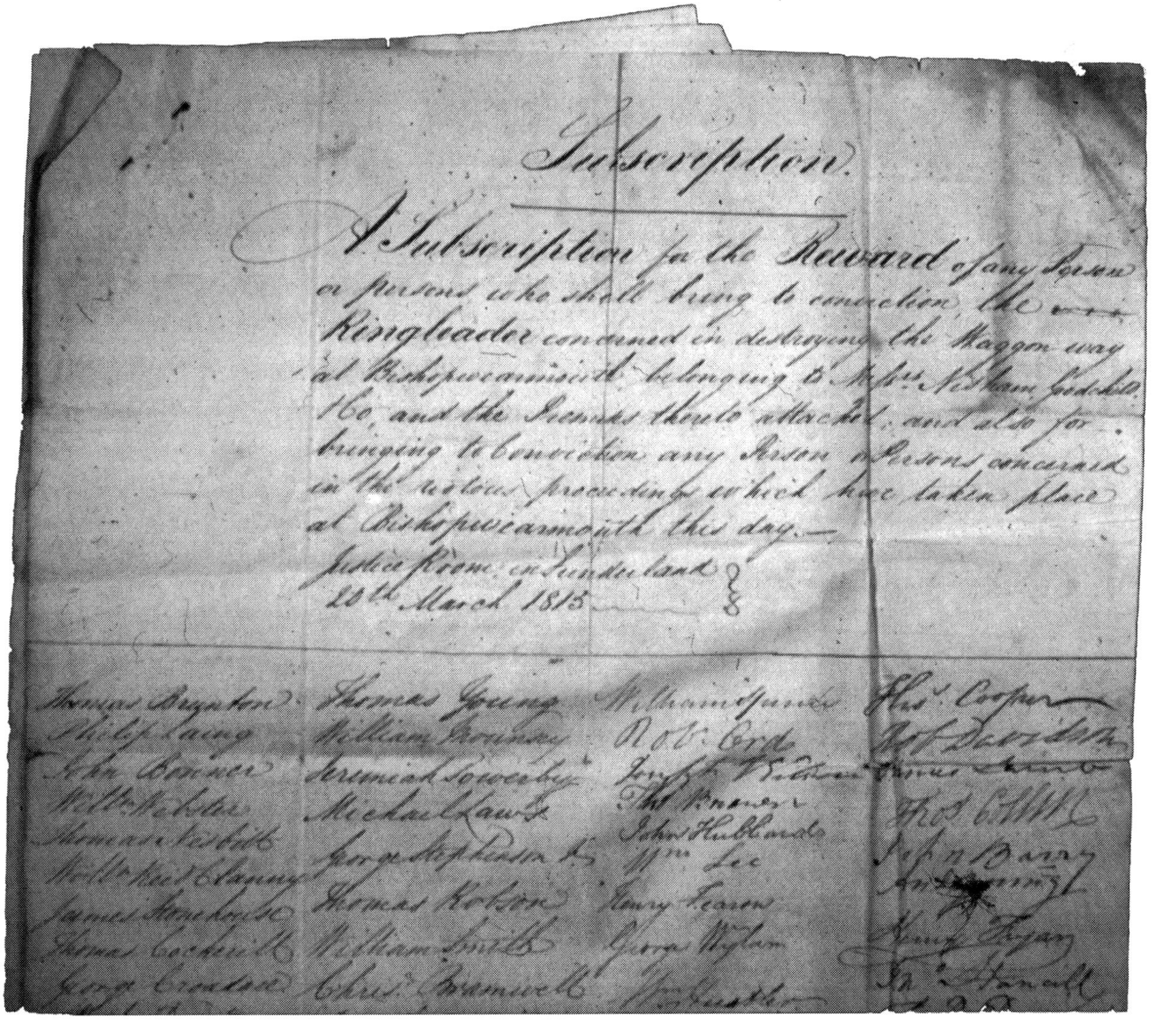

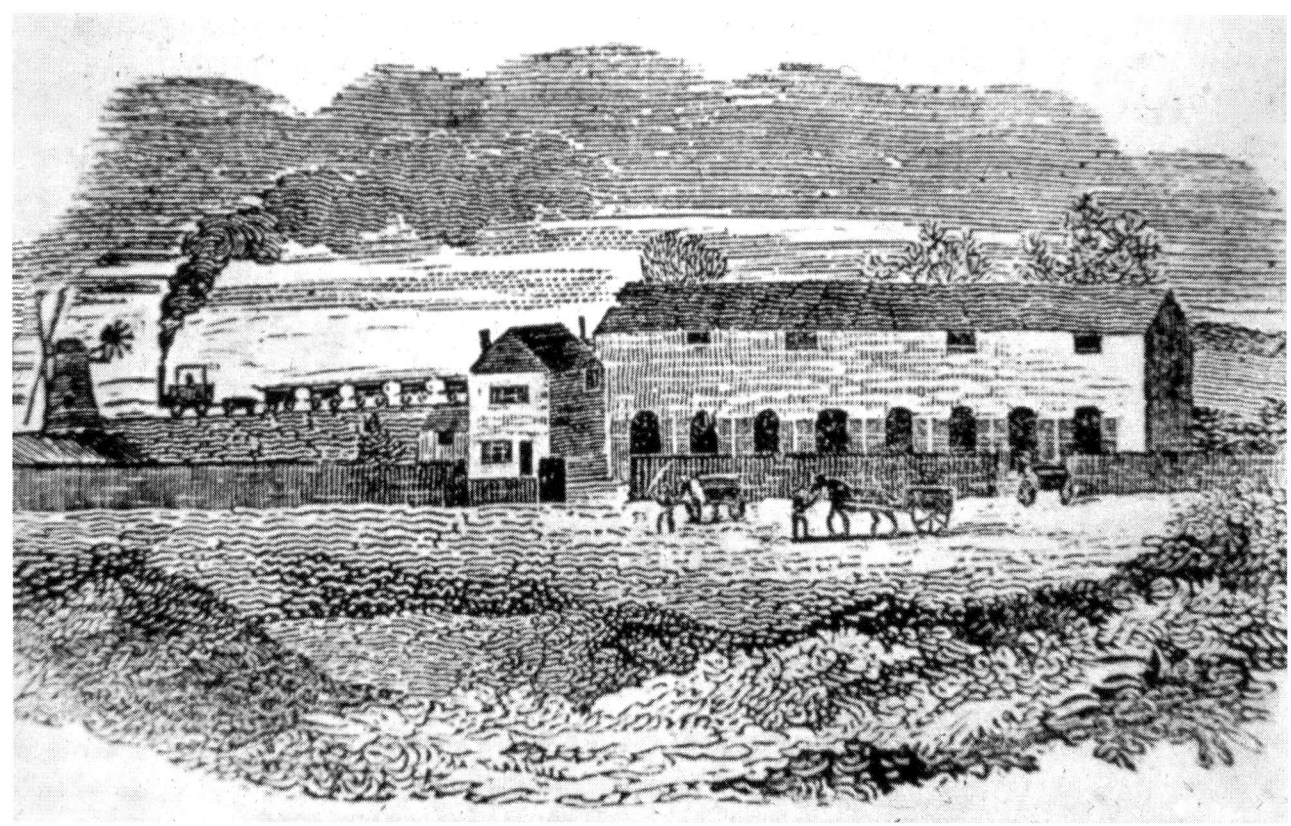

of a new railway age as it used locomotives at the Hetton and Sunderland ends of the line as well as rope haulage powered by stationary steam engines and self-acting inclines. Horse power was not involved. The Hetton Railway was also of national significance in being the first complete line engineered by George Stephenson (1781-1848); George's younger brother, Robert (1788-1837), supervized the construction of the line.

The Railway was far from satisfactory in its first years and sections of the line were radically altered. It then, however, became an outstanding success. After the output of the new pits at Elemore and Eppleton was added to that of Lyons, there were 180,000 chaldrons of coal (477,000 tons) travelling over the line by 1829, three times as much as the original estimate. To handle the demands of this traffic locomotives were replaced by rope haulage powered by stationary steam engines on the northern section of the line. The Hetton line was described as 'the finest in England' by two engineers from the Prussian Ministry of Mining who were studying English railways in 1826-1827.

In 1831 a third major colliery railway was opened on Wearside. The 3rd Marquis of Londonderry's (1776-1854) Rainton and Seaham Railway, engineered by John Buddle to the 4 feet 2 inch gauge, replaced an earlier line to staiths in the Penshaw area. It linked the Londonderry collieries at Rainton and Pittington to the Marquis's new dock at Seaham (*see map page 6*). Rope haulage by stationary steam engines or self-acting inclines was used. Both the Londonderry and Lambton lines were converted to the standard 4 feet 8½ inch gauge, which had been adopted by all the public railways in the North East, in 1843.

Until the 1830s all the railways in the Wearside area had been private lines constructed by the owners of collieries and quarries to carry minerals. They operated on the 'wayleave' system, paying landowners for crossing their property. The Stanhope and Tyne Railroad, which ran through the northern part of the area at Washington, also used wayleaves, but was a public

Illustrated heading from a bill issued by the Hetton Landsale in Chester Road, Sunderland. It shows one of George Stephenson's engines passing the depot where coal from the Hetton Company's collieries was sold for use in the town. The name landsale shows its purpose (as opposed to coal being sold to be shipped out to sea through the staiths). The Newbottle Railway had its coal depot close to its staiths. The date on the invoice is 26th August, 1839 during the period when this section of the Hetton line was worked by the Winter's Lane stationary engine (close to present day Meadowside). As, however, most of the date is handwritten, the invoice was presumably designed and printed during 1822-1827 when this section was still locomotive-worked.

railway (*see map page 6*). Thomas Harrison (1808-1888) was the Engineer, with George Stephenson's son Robert (1803-1859) as consulting engineer. From the quarries at Stanhope to South Shields it opened to freight in 1834 and passengers in 1835 it acted as a common carrier and conveyed passengers and general goods, although lime and coal were its main traffic. It obtained an Act of Parliament for its construction but was still built on a wayleave system. The line was worked by a mixture of horses, stationary engines, self-acting inclines and locomotives.

The Stanhope and Tyne was followed by the Durham and Sunderland Railway (DSR), the first section of which opened in 1836 (*see map page 6*). It also was authorized by Act of Parliament but made use of wayleaves. The DSR had the transport of coal as its main objective and the Durham terminus was not in the city, but just outside in Shincliffe because this was close to collieries which the railway served. A branch from Murton ran to Haswell. The Sunderland passenger station was a basic wooden structure on the Town Moor, en route to staiths which the DSR built on Low Quay. Passenger carriages were originally attached to coal trains, but later formed their own trains. The Durham and Sunderland was promoted by leading figures in Sunderland, such as Andrew White, the Borough's first mayor in 1835, Edward Backhouse, the Quaker banker, and Philip Laing, the shipbuilder.

The Engineer for the Durham and Sunderland was Thomas Emerson Forster (1802-1875) who was not connected with the 'Stephenson school' and felt a railway should be operated by powered inclines. It was the longest public railway in Britain worked by stationary steam engines. It was also the last of the lines on Wearside built from 1812 which used rope working, either by stationary engines or on self-acting inclines. Rope working has tended to be overlooked in the history of Sunderland's

Detail from Mark Thompson's painting of the Opening of Sunderland South Dock in 1850 which shows, on the skyline above the Dock walls, the wooden Durham and Sunderland Railway station (*left*) and its Sunderland engine house (*far right*). Until the Dock opened the DSR continued to the staiths at Low Quay on the River Wear.

Lithograph from Thomas Hair's *Sketches of the Coal Mines of Northumberland and Durham*. It is taken from Hair's watercolour of about 1838 and shows the Durham and Sunderland Railway's Pittington stationary engine, with its drums for rope haulage, and also a passenger train.

The Victoria Bridge photographed about 1880. North Biddick Colliery, with its staiths, can be seen to the right through the arches of the bridge (*see map pages 6 & 7*). The bridge took its name from the fact it was opened on Queen Victoria's coronation day on 20th June, 1838. It later carried East Coast Main Line trains until the Team Valley route was completed in 1872.

The Development of Sunderland's Railways: The Colliery Railways and the First Public Railways 1812 – 1840

The Brandling Junction Railway's Wearmouth station behind the present-day Roker Avenue in Monkwearmouth. It was a basic wooden structure in which Richard Lowery said in 1839: 'the usual accommodation provided for civilized people was entirely wanting at this, as at almost every other Brandling Junction Railway station'. It was due to be replaced by a permanent station near the Wheatsheaf Inn, but the 1839 building was in fact superseded by Monkwearmouth station in North Bridge Street.

railways. Even, however, the Hetton Colliery Railway, best known for Stephenson's locomotives, used rope haulage and self-acting inclines for much of its route. Many of the ropes, made first from hemp and then from wire, came from ropeworks in Sunderland. These works also supplied ropes for railways further afield, such as the Stockton and Darlington.

Wearside's next public line was the Durham Junction Railway (DJR), promoted by the directors of the Stanhope and Tyne Railroad (STR) to link the STR at Washington with the projected Durham branch of the Hartlepool Dock Railway. The latter was not, however, completed beyond Haswell and the DJR terminated close to collieries at Rainton Meadows (*see map page 6*). The Durham Junction, engineered, like the STR, by Thomas Harrison, with James Walker (1781-1862) as the consulting engineer, was notable for the Victoria Bridge across the River Wear. It was entirely locomotive worked and opened to freight in 1838 and passengers in 1840.

A direct railway link between the Tyne and the Wear was provided in 1839 by Brandling Junction Railway from Gateshead to South Shields and Monkwearmouth (*see map page 6*). It was promoted by the brothers John and Robert Brandling and surveyed by George Stephenson. Although they obtained an Act of Parliament, the land was acquired under the wayleave system; much of it was already owned by the Brandlings. South of Brockley Whins station the railway crossed the Stanhope and Tyne Railway on the level and connections were made to allow the exchange of traffic between the two lines. While it was mainly locomotive worked, a stationary engine was used on the final section of the branch to the dock on the north side of the Wear which had been opened by the Wearmouth Dock Company in 1837.

The Hudson Era and the Docks 1841 - 1855

None of the public railways which were established in the 1830s were financially successful. The Stanhope and Tyne, £440,000 in deficit at the end of 1840, was wound up in 1841 and was succeeded by the Pontop and South Shields Railway. The Durham and Sunderland Railway, Durham Junction Railway, Brandling Junction Railway and the Wearmouth Dock were also disappointments to their shareholders. To stay in business in 1841 the Durham and Sunderland had to ask the landowners for a reduction in the wayleaves they charged the company and the colliery owners for an increase in the dues they paid.

In 1841 the Newcastle and Darlington Junction Railway was formed to link the Great North of England Railway (which ran from York to Darlington) with the Durham Junction Railway at Rainton, thus completing the route from York to Newcastle. The Chairman was George Hudson (1800-1871). A York draper and Lord Mayor of that city, Hudson was to become known as the 'Railway King' in the late 1840s when he controlled lines stretching from Berwick to Bristol and Colchester.

Hudson's Newcastle and Darlington Junction was completed in 1844 when it also took over the Durham Junction. The Brandling Junction was purchased the following year.

In 1841 Hudson was asked to stand as an MP by the Sunderland Tory party who were anxious to break the Liberal monopoly of the town's two Parliamentary seats which had existed since they were created in 1832. It was realised that Hudson's railway influence could greatly benefit the town.

George Hudson was duly elected in 1845 and in 1846 the Durham and

Lithograph of Monkwearmouth station when first opened in 1848 'respectfully dedicated to George Hudson'. The *Sunderland Herald* wrote that it was 'a great ornament to the town and a credit to all concerned in its erection'.

The Development of Sunderland's Railways: The Hudson Era and the Docks 1841 - 1855

Portrait of George Hudson 'The Railway King' by Sir Francis Grant. It was probably commissioned by Hudson's South Dock Company. It later hung in the offices of the River Wear Commissioners and then at Monkwearmouth Station Museum. It is now on display at Sunderland Museum, Library and Winter Gardens.

Election card for one of George Hudson's Parliamentary campaigns in Sunderland.

Sunderland Railway and the Wearmouth Dock Company's North Dock, were purchased by the Newcastle and Darlington Junction Railway (NDJR) on terms which were extremely favourable to their shareholders. The NDJR changed its name first to the York and Newcastle Railway and then to the York, Newcastle and Berwick Railway in 1847.

Two developments in the town of Sunderland resulted from Hudson's election as MP. The inadequate Brandling Junction building was replaced in 1848 by the new Monkwearmouth station. This was built in a far more impressive style than would otherwise have been the case because Hudson wished to mark his election as a Sunderland MP.

The second result of Hudson's election had a massive impact on the economy of Sunderland. This was the construction of a new dock on the south side of the Wear by the Sunderland Dock Company, of which Hudson was the Chairman, and to which his Newcastle and Darlington Junction Railway contributed.

The construction of the South Dock was necessary if Sunderland was to continue to be a major coal shipping town. With port improvements at Seaham, Hartlepool and Middlesbrough and the limitations of the tidal North Dock apparent, it was clear that there was a need for a non-tidal dock to reduce overcrowding in the river.

The South Dock, served by the Durham and Sunderland line, was opened on 20th June, 1850. By this time George Hudson had been removed from his railway chairmanships as details of his dubious financial dealings emerged. Among the charges brought against him were that finance from the Newcastle and Darlington Junction Railway had been invested in the South Dock without proper Parliamentary authority. Hudson's promotion of the Dock meant that he remained a popular figure for 10 years after his national disgrace. He only lost his Parliamentary seat in 1859 when the financial problems of the South Dock became apparent.

Coal traffic through the South Dock increased after the Penshaw branch from the then main line to Hendon Junction was opened for freight in 1852 and for passengers in 1853. The Sunderland passenger terminus in Burdon Road was named after the nearby Fawcett Street area which was developing as the commercial centre of Sunderland. The passenger service ran from here to Durham (Gilesgate), but from 1857 it went over the new Bishop Auckland branch from Leamside to the present Durham station. Most trains ran through to Bishop Auckland.

In 1854 the York, Newcastle and Berwick Railway amalgamated with other companies to form the North Eastern Railway (NER) which was to dominate the region for 70 years. The colliery railways still, however, continued to play an important part on Wearside. Indeed, also in in 1854 the 3rd Marquis of Londonderry opened the Seaham and Sunderland Railway to staiths at the South Dock as the dock he had built at Seaham could not cope with the output of the Londonderry and South Hetton collieries. Unlike the other lines built by colliery owners, it was a public railway and carried passengers between Seaham Harbour and a station at Hendon Burn. In 1859 a link was built between the new Ryhope Colliery and the Londonderry Railway which took Ryhope's coal to

Thomas Elliot Harrison (1808-1888) was one of the North-East's finest railway engineers. Brought up in Sunderland, he became the civil engineer for the Stanhope and Tyne Railway, working under Robert Stephenson, and then the Engineer for the Durham Junction Railway, including the Victoria Bridge. He became the Engineer for George Hudson's railways, such as the Penshaw line. He was instrumental in the formation of the North Eastern Railway and was briefly its General Manager before concentrating his efforts as its civil engineer and on his private consultancy. His NER work included Durham viaduct, York station and the Monkwearmouth Junction line in Sunderland. He was President of the Institute of Civil Engineers. His nephew, Charles, designed the Queen Alexandra Bridge when he was Consultant Engineer to the NER.

Ryhope Colliery at the time of its opening in 1859. The tender locomotive would have belonged to the Londonderry Railway which worked colliery traffic from their line from Seaham to South Dock. The 0-6-0ST was most probably the Ryhope Coal Company's engine and housed in the engine shed on the left.

the South Dock.

Despite the extra coal which came over the Londonderry Railway, the South Dock Company was unsuccessful. The River Wear Commissioners, who controlled the river, were able to levy a toll on every vessel leaving the Dock, thus making the company uneconomic. As a result, the South Dock Company was taken over by the Commissioners in 1860. The new Hendon Dock was added to the existing (renamed) Hudson Dock in 1868. It was claimed for many years in Sunderland that, because the NER had no financial interest in the South Docks, it tried to reroute coal traffic though Sunderland to the docks it owned at Hartlepool and Tyne Dock. The small tidal North Dock at Sunderland was owned by the North Eastern Railway; its main traffic was the import of timber. It was of so little importance that the NER was content to pass control of the North Dock over to the River Wear Commissioners in 1922.

The North Eastern Railway 1855 - 1899

During the first 20 years after the formation of the North Eastern Railway in 1854 no major addition was made to railways in the Sunderland area, although construction of a new main line through Durham led to London to Newcastle trains being diverted onto that route in 1872. The railway through Washington was henceforth known as 'The Old Main Line.' The Stanhope and Tyne route on Wearside now became purely a freight line.

Various improvements were made to the NER system. Rope haulage was successively abandoned on the Durham and Sunderland line between 1850 and 1860. Three years later the Town Moor station, which was now in the midst of an area used for coal traffic, was replaced by a new station at Hendon. From 1868 Londonderry Railway trains also used this station in place of their Hendon Burn passenger terminus.

The 2nd Earl of Durham (1828-1879) decided to abandon his rope-operated railway east of the colliery at Herrington. Lambton trains were locomotive hauled over the Penshaw branch first by a link from Millfield to the existing line at Hylton Road, then from 1865 via a new line via Deptford and a tunnel to the staiths. The Lambton Railway also obtained running powers to the staiths at the South Dock.

The 1870s saw further railway building in Sunderland. The Hylton, Southwick and Monkwearmouth Railway of 1876 linked Monkwearmouth to the Pontop and South Shields line near Washington (*see map page 7*). It was promoted by the owners of the industries along the route rather than the NER and this is shown by the engineer being the firm of Meik and Nisbet rather than Thomas Harrison. Thomas Meik (1812-1896) had been the River Wear Commissioners (RWC) Engineer until 1868 when he set

Poster, probably produced during the 1865 general election, showing (*second left with cigar*) James Hartley, Conservative MP from 1865 – 1868 and (*far right*) most probably George Hudson, Hartley's only predecessor as a Tory MP for Sunderland. The setting is Fawcett Street station, with Mowbray Park in the background. The platform awning shown here was moved, after the closure of Fawcett Street in 1879, to Morpeth station where it still survives. The cartoon shows a NER seat with 'serpent' supports. James Hartley (1811 – 1886), a major glassmaker was a Director of the NER from 1856 and was said to be influential in bringing about the construction of the Monkwearmouth Junction Railway. On Hartley's death Sir James Laing, the shipbuilder, became a Director until 1902.

Looking north from High Street West along Pann Lane during the building of the Sunderland north tunnel by the 'cut and cover' method in about 1877. The façade of the public house, on the left, and the back of St Mary's Church, on the right, still survive. The photograph shows the major work involved in the construction of the Monkwearmouth Junction Railway which necessitated the demolition of many buildings including the original Elephant Tea House which had stood in the foreground. The North Eastern Railway provided the sites and finance for replacement properties. The replacement Tea House, on the opposite side of High Street and which was until recently a bank, was designed by Frank Caws (1846-1905), an inventive Sunderland architect. Caws had previously worked for the NER and claimed that he had originally proposed the route of the Monkwearmouth Junction Railway.

up his own practice with William Nisbet (1837-1897), his assistant at the RWC. Nisbet laid out the railway and supervised its construction by direct labour rather than contractors. Once completed, the line was worked by the North Eastern Railway which took over the company in 1883.

The major Sunderland railway project in the second half of the 19th century was the Monkwearmouth Junction Railway which linked the railway systems on the north and south banks of the Wear (*see map pages 7 & 8*). It ran from Monkwearmouth station to the existing lines to the south at Ryhope Grange and involved major construction work, including a bridge across the Wear, two tunnels, and a new central station.

The opening of the Monkwearmouth Junction line in 1879 transformed the Sunderland railway scene. Of the three former termini, Fawcett Street and Hendon were closed and Monkwearmouth became a through station for local trains. Not only, were coal trains from North of the Wear able to reach the South Docks, but Sunderland gained long distance express passenger trains running from Newcastle to Leeds, Manchester and London.

With the opening of the Monkwearmouth Junction line, the North Eastern Railway in Sunderland settled down to a period of relative prosperity which was to last for a quarter of a century. Several of the NER

stations, such as Millfield, Pallion and Ryhope were rebuilt during this time, sometimes in connection with alterations to the lines they served. The goods warehouse at Monkwearmouth was extended in the 1870s, 1890s and 1900s, reflecting its role as the main depot for general goods on Wearside. Separate offices and stables were also built at Monkwearmouth.

In contrast to the expansion of the North Eastern, the wagonways to the Wear contracted as collieries and quarries were either worked out or connected to the main line system. A major reduction in the private colliery railway mileage came in 1896 when the 6th Marquis of Londonderry (1852-1915) closed the Rainton and Seaham line west of Seaham Colliery as the pits at the western end of the line ceased production.

The Wearmouth Bridge, designed by Thomas Harrison, which was said to be the 'largest Hog-Back iron girder in the world' when opened in 1879. This photograph of an NER local train crossing the bridge, probably taken about 1900, also shows the Lambton Staiths in the foreground and the Wearmouth iron bridge, rebuilt by Robert Stephenson in 1859, in the background.

The opening of the new No. 19 staith at the South Docks in 1890. The first vessel to be loaded was the *Melbourne* which had been built by Pickersgill and engineered by George Clark, both on the Wear, earlier in the year. After taking on 5,600 tons she left for Genoa. In the new staith coal was delivered to the hold of the ship through spouts instead of the earlier drops where wagons were lowered on platforms. The NER 10 ton wagons in the photograph were replacing chaldron wagons on the Railway's system.

The North Eastern and the Colliery Railways 1900 - 1922

By the beginning of the 20th century railways had become the lifeblood of Wearside's industries. Coal, and almost all the other freight going out by sea, was first moved to the South Docks and the Lambton and Hetton Staiths by rail. Most of the raw material for the local industries, such as the steel for shipyards, arrived in Sunderland by rail.

In the 1900s the North Eastern Railway system on Wearside expanded again. The NER had obtained powers for a railway between Seaham and Sunderland and in 1900 purchased the Londonderry Railway's Seaham and Sunderland section. This was opened in 1905 and some of the trains which had previously run via Seaton were diverted by the new route. The part of the Londonderry Railway between Ryhope and Silksworth Collieries was retained under Londonderry ownership, but was worked by the NER.

Another major, and costly, expansion was being planned by the NER in 1900. Due to the increasing movement of coal to the South Docks, the Railway was drawing up plans for a second crossing of the Wear at Sunderland.

While the vast majority of coal was shipped through the staiths to locations on the East Coast, such as the London gasworks, some wagons went to landsales for use in the local area for domestic and commercial use. These coal depots were situated at most North Eastern stations and also at various points on the Lambton and Hetton Railways. The latter two companies also found new outlets for their coal in the new electricity generation stations of the area. The Hetton line served the Sunderland Corporation Electricity Works at Hylton Road, opened in 1900, while the Lambton Collieries owned the generating station at Philadelphia, opened in 1905.

Other developments on the two colliery railways included the re-routing of the Hetton line between the Barnes and the staiths in the late 1890s and 1900s, which resulted in tunnels at the Barnes and Hylton Road and bridges over Eden Vale and Chester Road. This removed the need for level crossings over roads. On the Lambton Railway, after acquisition from the 3rd Earl of Durham (1855-1928) by Sir James Joicey (1846-1936) in 1896, improvements included modernization and extension of the Lambton Staiths.

In 1911 Sir James Joicey also acquired the Hetton Company. The now-amalgamated Lambton and Hetton systems were linked by a sharply curved tunnel between the two sets of staiths at Sunderland. A connecting

A train of empty coal wagons crosses Silksworth Lane in the 1890s/early 1900s headed by a Hetton Colliery 0-6-0ST, probably No. 4 (built as an 0-6-0 by Robert Stephenson, 1865, and rebuilt as an 0-6-0ST at Hetton). The level crossings here and at Durham Road disappeared when the line was rerouted under the Barnes tunnel.

The extension to Doxford's Pallion Shipyard under construction in 1903 showing the 0-6-0ST *Alexandra* (Manning, Wardle, 1901) which belonged to the contractors Walter Scott and Middleton. This view shows the zig-zag which was necessary to reach the Deptford branch.

link was also later built between Rainton Meadows and Rainton Bridge on course of the former Londonderry Railway.

While coal was all-important for the railways, other industries contributed traffic from Sunderland. This was particularly the case with the Fulwell Lime Works, while glass and rope works also generated railway traffic from the town.

A significant amount of goods traffic arrived at the Docks for onward transport by railway. At the North Dock, this was timber, but at the South Docks the wide variety of freight imports included iron ore, which was moved by train to the Consett Steelworks, and oil. Other goods unloaded at the Docks were processed by the town's industries with the finished products also leaving by railway. Esparto grass left as paper and grain as flour.

Inward traffic by rail was particularly important in the case of shipbuilding, where steel plates and angles were received from Jarrow, Consett and Teesside. It was not possible for some shipyards to have railway connections and the steel for those on the north bank was unloaded in the goods yard at Monkwearmouth. On the south bank, the shipyards were well below the Penshaw and Deptford branches. In 1898 Short's Shipyard constructed a semi-circular branch from Pallion station (which had to be rebuilt to accommodate it. The neighbouring Doxford's shipyard, which already had a zig-zag to overcome the height problems, greatly extended its yard and railway system.

Many other Sunderland firms had their own sidings, although built at far less cost. This can be seen from the three intermediate stations on the Penshaw branch in 1904. Millfield had sidings to two coal landsales, a flour

An NER '398' class 0-6-0 stands with wagons in the sidings of Chapman's Steam Bakery at Millfield in about 1900. Within a ¾ mile radius of Millfield station there were 20 private sidings.

One of several postcards produced during the construction of the Queen Alexandra Bridge. It was then known as 'The New Wear Bridge', as it was only on the opening by the Earl of Durham on 10th June, 1909 that it was it revealed that the Queen had agreed to it being named after her. The centre span of the two-level bridge contained 2,600 tons of steel and was the heaviest in Britain at the time.

mill, a bakery, a slate yard, glassworks and a cask yard. Pallion had 15 private sidings including several forges and the recent shipyard connections. Hylton had five private sidings serving Ford Paper Works, Ford Limestone Quarry and Brickworks, Bagnall's Forge and Engine Works, Reay and Usher's Forge and Offerton coal depot.

There were also significant passenger services on Wearside. In addition to local trains to Newcastle, South Shields, Hartlepool, Bishop Auckland via Durham and Durham (Elvet) via Hetton, there were long distance trains from Sunderland to Manchester and Liverpool via York. From 1905 the Liverpool trains used the new Durham Coast route via Seaham.

As well as providing a direct route from Sunderland to Hartlepool the Durham Coast line generated new traffic from the intermediate stations and, more importantly, from the collieries that were being sunk at Easington and Horden. The NER would almost certainly have considered its investment worthwhile. This was not to be the case with the other major infrastructure expenditure in the area in the 1900s – the Queen Alexandra Bridge.

The bridge and its approach lines from Diamond Hall Junction, on the Penshaw line, and Castletown Junction, on the Hylton, Southwick and Monkwearmouth branch, was opened in 1909. This enabled coal trains from the Stanhope and Tyne line to run directly to the South Dock without reversal at Washington and Penshaw. The bridge was designed by Charles Harrison (1848-1916), nephew of Thomas and the NER's consultant engineer. It was a massive two-tier structure, the lower deck used for a road link between Pallion and Southwick.

The cost of the construction of the bridge and its rail and road approaches was stated to be around £450,000, with Sunderland Corporation's contribution being about £200,000 and Southwick Council £11,000 on account of the road deck. The Railway contributed the major amount. The Corporation was criticized for the amount of its expenditure, but, in the event, it certainly had the better bargain as only one coal train a day ran over the bridge until the early 1920s when regular traffic appears to have ceased.

When construction of the Queen Alexandra Bridge was planned in 1900 it seemed likely that the coal output being shipped through Sunderland would continue. The River Wear Commissioners were building two new outer piers to make entry into the Docks easier for colliers. 1904 was a record year for coal shipment from Sunderland – 5,117,230 tons – but thereafter the amount dropped. The River Wear Commissioners stopped work on their new South Pier and the trade recession led to a decline in shipbuilding orders. Another factor which worked against the Queen Alexandra Bridge by the time it opened in 1909 was that the centres of coal production were continuing to move eastwards. This is shown by new collieries being sunk adjacent to the Durham Coast line.

The NER remained of major commercial importance in Sunderland. This was reflected in the construction of new offices at Burdon House in 1916. They were designed by the NER's architect, William Bell, who had also designed the Central station and the stables at Monkwearmouth. The ground floor was let out as shops.

Burdon House opened two years after the outbreak of the First World War. This impacted on railway traffic which arrived or left Sunderland by sea. It also meant that railway staff joined the forces. For the duration of the war women undertook some of the men's duties, such as porters.

Sunderland escaped the bombardment of Scarborough, Whitby and Hartlepool, but on 1st April, 1916 a Zeppelin dropped high explosive bombs which caused deaths and injuries, particularly in the Monkwearmouth area where the goods warehouse roof and other buildings were damaged.

First World War memorial from the offices of Monkwearmouth goods station. The DLI (Durham Light Infantry) was a local regiment while the Northumberland Fusiliers had a 'Pals' battalion formed from NER staff.

SUNDERLAND'S RAILWAYS

The LNER 1923 - 1947

As part of the Railway Grouping the North Eastern Railway became incorporated in the London and North Eastern Railway (LNER) in 1923. It faced new challenges as the railways in the Sunderland area were beginning to experience road competition for passenger traffic. Previously the Sunderland Corporation Tramways had only passed the main station and those at Millfield and Monkwearmouth and had little impact on the NER.

The Sunderland and District Tramways, whose routes served Hetton and Penshaw and other locations where there were North Eastern stations would have taken some passengers away from the trains, but it was the motor buses that were introduced after the First World War that had an impact on the trains. The Sunderland District Company replaced its trams by buses in 1924. The Northern General and United Companies introduced several routes as did other smaller operators; in 1923 W.H. Jolly started a service from South Hylton to link with the Corporation tramways at Pallion.

Motor transport also began to abstract some of the smaller goods traffic but the railways were still the predominant carrier for Sunderland's industries and only they could carry the bulk mineral traffic of coal. Nevertheless, the production of coal was beginning to drop and, with the Queen Alexandra Bridge no longer in use, the Hylton, Southwick and

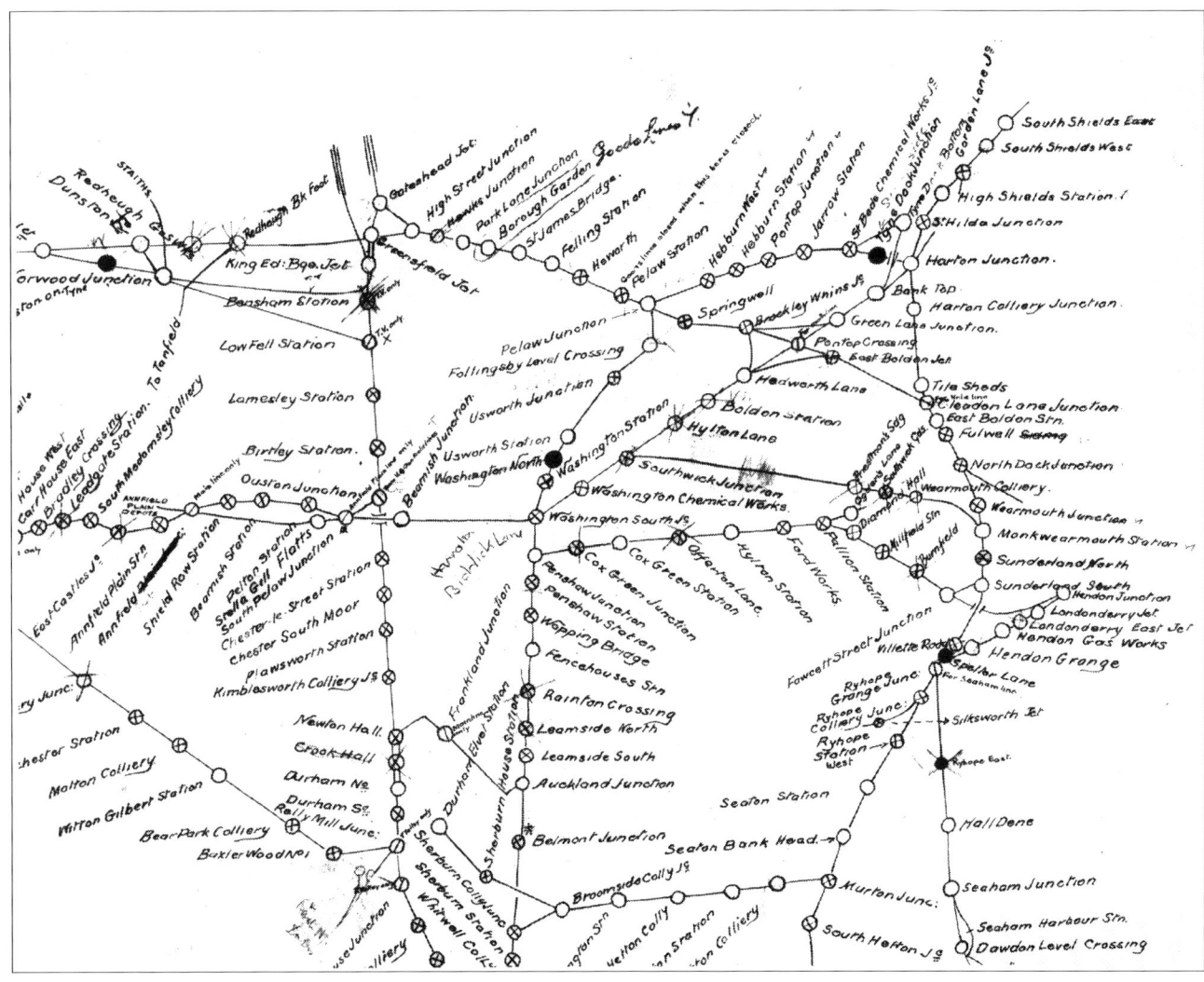

Diagram showing the many signal boxes in the Wearside area during the LNER era when the Queen Alexandra Bridge had ceased to be used. The boxes marked with a cross could be switched out to save staff during quieter periods, such as at night. The signal boxes with level crossings could not be switched out during the hours when trains were running. After boxes had been permanently closed they were marked black on the diagram.

'V3' class 2-6-2T No. 7634 at Washington station in the late 1940s. The locomotive is one of a class the LNER introduced to the area in 1935. In contrast, the coaches are NER clerestory vehicles.

Monkwearmouth line was closed west of Hylton Colliery.

Expansion of the passenger facilities in Sunderland took place when the LNER opened Seaburn station in 1937 at Fulwell because of the growing number of houses in the vicinity and the development of nearby Seaburn as a seaside resort. It also superseded the football platform at Forfar Street.

The NER locomotives and rolling stock used on express passenger and freight trains were replaced by new LNER types and for some years new steam railcars were used for a few local services. NER locomotives continued to predominate, however, on local passenger and mineral trains until the 1950s and 1960s when they were replaced by diesels.

The LNER's years in control of Sunderland's railways was overshadowed by the Second World War. This had some of the same effect on the railways as in 1914-1918, but there was the added impact of the German bombing campaign aimed at the shipyards and docks. Sunderland was the most heavily bombed town in England north of Hull. The major damage to the railway infrastructure was caused on September 1940 when a bomb destroyed part of the Sunderland station roof.

Clearing up work after the German bomb damage to Sunderland station on 6th September, 1940. A carriage bogie was blown through the window of Joseph's Sports Shop in Union Street. The LNER refused to remove the wheels and the ARP only agreed to do so if they were indemnified against possible damage to the shop.

'D20' class 4-4-0 No. 62372 at Sunderland station with a train for Hartlepool in 1955. The platform awnings first installed after the bomb damage and then extended after the complete removal of the roof in 1952 can be seen. The end of the sign over the shop of B. Joseph and Son can be seen in the top left of the photograph. This was where the bogie of a carriage had ended up after the 1940 bombing

British Railways and the National Coal Board 1948 - 1994

The LNER was nationalized and became part of British Railways (BR) in 1948. The previous year nationalization had led to the Lambton, Hetton and Joicey and other coal companies being incorporated in the National Coal Board (NCB) in 1947.

The LNER's plan for a reconstruction of Sunderland station, which would have included a hotel, did not proceed. The construction of a new entrance at the south end and complete replacement of the overall roof by umbrella canopies in 1953 were the only significant development.

Changes to the railway network began in 1952 and 1953 with the closure of the stations on the former Durham and Sunderland Railway route via Seaton. Most of another of Wearside's early railways – the Hetton Colliery – closed in 1959 after the opening of the Hawthorn Combined Mine, to which coal was sent underground from Elemore and Eppleton Collieries.

The 1950s saw the start of the replacement of steam by diesel motive power. Diesel multiple units were introduced on Newcastle – Middlesbrough passenger services in 1955. The other local trains were dieselized in the next few years. Diesel locomotives also superseded steam engines on express trains and on shunting and goods duties in the 1950s and 1960s. The dieselization of coal traffic in 1967 marked the end of steam in the North-East of England. The NCB also replaced their steam locomotives by diesels in the 1950s – 1970s.

Dismantling No.2 self-acting incline between Warden Law and North Moor on the Hetton Colliery Railway on 25th November, 1959.

Class '40' No. D250 pilots 'A3' 4-6-2 No. 60065 *Knight of Thistle* on a Newcastle to London via Sunderland Sunday train on 7th May, 1961 during the changeover from steam to diesel traction. The train is photographed approaching Ryhope Grange shortly before being diverted by Wellfield. It is double-headed because of the steep climb up Seaton Bank.

The contraction of the passenger services on Wearside was most marked between 1963 and 1965 when services were withdrawn from the 'Old Main Line' from Sunderland via the Penshaw branch to Durham and Bishop Auckland and to South Shields, along with the stopping trains to West Hartlepool.

By 1967 Seaburn and Sunderland (the latter modernized in in 1965) were the sole stations which retained their passenger services. The Newcastle – Middlesbrough route was converted to pay-train operation in 1969 with tickets being issued by guards on all local trains. Only Sunderland retained its booking office.

The contraction of the freight services, both on the BR and NCB networks, was even more dramatic than that of the passenger services. The goods yards were shut in the 1960s and 1970s apart from Monkwearmouth goods station which closed in 1981. BR traffic to coal merchants' depots ceased in 1984

Reduction in coal output brought the end of NCB locomotives working over the Penshaw branch and closure of the Lambton Staiths in 1967. A year later the Wearmouth Colliery Staiths, the last on the river banks, ceased to be used for coal. By the late 1960s the movement of coal from pit to staith by colliery locomotives, a major feature of the Sunderland railway scene, had therefore ended. The lines to Ryhope, Silksworth, Hylton and Houghton Collieries closed with their pits in the 1960s and 1970s.

A Sunderland to Durham Metro-Cammell diesel multiple unit approaches Pallion station on 22nd April, 1963, a year before withdrawal of passenger services. NCB 0-6-2T No. 30 (Kitson, 1907) is waiting to come off the Deptford branch and follow the passenger train to Cox Green Junction.

Four 'Pacer' four-wheel diesel multiple units on a return football special from Middlesbrough to Seaburn near Ryhope Grange on 27th August 1989.The first and last two units are class '143' units (the last two painted Tyne and Wear Passenger Transport Executive yellow and white livery were among the six purchased by the County Council in 1983), The '143's were later transferred away from the North East. The second unit is one of the inferior class 142s, members of which are, unfortunately, still in use on Wearside in the late 2010s.

From 1974 passenger services between Sunderland and Newcastle were subsidized by Tyne and Wear County Council through the Passenger Transport Executive. This resulted in an increase in the number of trains to Newcastle. When the County Council was abolished in 1986 transport powers passed to the Tyne and Wear Passenger Transport Authority and later to the North East Combined Authority.

In contrast to the improvement in the service to Newcastle, was the loss during the 1960s and 1970s of the surviving long distance express trains which were diverted away from the route via Sunderland to the East Coast Main line; the last was the Sunday-only Newcastle – London train which was re-routed in 1977. There was a revival in 1985 of a through service, *The Cleveland Express*, to London via Sunderland and Middlesbrough, but this ceased before privatization.

The 1980s saw major changes to the movement of coal by rail on Wearside. The Herrington and Philadelphia sections of the Lambton system closed in 1984 and 1985 and the branch to the Lambton Coke Works at Fencehouses in 1986. In that year the National Coal Board became known as British Coal.

Class '37' No. 37198 passes Monkwearmouth station on 10th April, 1985 with a train of unfitted and vacuum-fitted wagons for Wearmouth Colliery. These wagons were being phased out and many awaiting scrapping are in the sidings on the right.

Class '56' No. 56112 leaving Wearmouth Colliery with air-braked wagons on 14th April, 1987. These were the final type of motive power and wagons used on trains from Wearside. Wearmouth was the last of the areas' collieries when it closed in 1993. This area is now occupied by Sunderland AFC's Stadium of Light.

On the British Railways system unbraked and vacuum-braked coal wagons were replaced by larger air-braked wagons. The last unbraked coal wagons were phased out in 1985. One of their last uses had been to Sunderland's domestic coal depots, all latterly concentrated on the stub of the Penshaw branch, but this traffic ceased in 1984.

Up until the mid-1980s Sunderland South dock remained an important shipping point for coal being transported to electricity power stations in the South-East of England. In 1983 1,570,529 tons of coal were shipped from South Dock, but the opening in 1985 of the new coal handling facilities at Tyne Dock, with the facility to handle larger vessels, led to a significant reduction and then the end of the South Docks' coal traffic.

By the mid 1980s only Wearmouth Colliery survived in Sunderland. Power stations in Yorkshire or the Tyne Dock Coal terminal were the destination of most of its coal. Wearmouth, the last colliery in the Durham coalfield, ceased production in 1993. The last part of the Durham and Sunderland line closed in 1993 after Murton Colliery ceased production and its stockpile cleared. South Dock motive power depot, which now only provided locomotives for coal traffic, closed in 1994. Sunderland's direct railway links with coal traffic now disappeared.

A Passenger Railway 1995 - 2018

From 1995 the only regular freight trains which passed through the City were from the Tyne Coal Terminal and were carrying imported coal to power stations, although there were other workings such as those from the nuclear power station at Hartlepool to Sellafield.

The mid-1990s also saw the privatization of British Railways with Railtrack taking over the infrastructure and English Welsh and Scottish Railways the freight operation in 1996. Regional Railways North East was franchised, first to MTL under the brand name of Northern Spirit; the company was taken over by Sunderland-based Arriva in 2000. As part of the larger Northern Rail franchise it was operated by Serco-Abellio until 2016 when Arriva took over again. There have been no long-term improvements since privatization in train services operated by these companies through Sunderland, with an additional service to Hartlepool only operating for a few years. In 2018, the rolling stock on the one-per-hour service from Teesside to Hexham still remains the 'Pacer' and 'Sprinter' trains introduced by British Railways in the mid-1980s.

The passenger service from Sunderland has, however, been transformed outside the franchise service by the extension of the Tyne and Wear Metro to South Hylton and the introduction of the Grand Central service to London. The Metro extension has indeed been the most important development in the railways of the City (which Sunderland became in 1992)

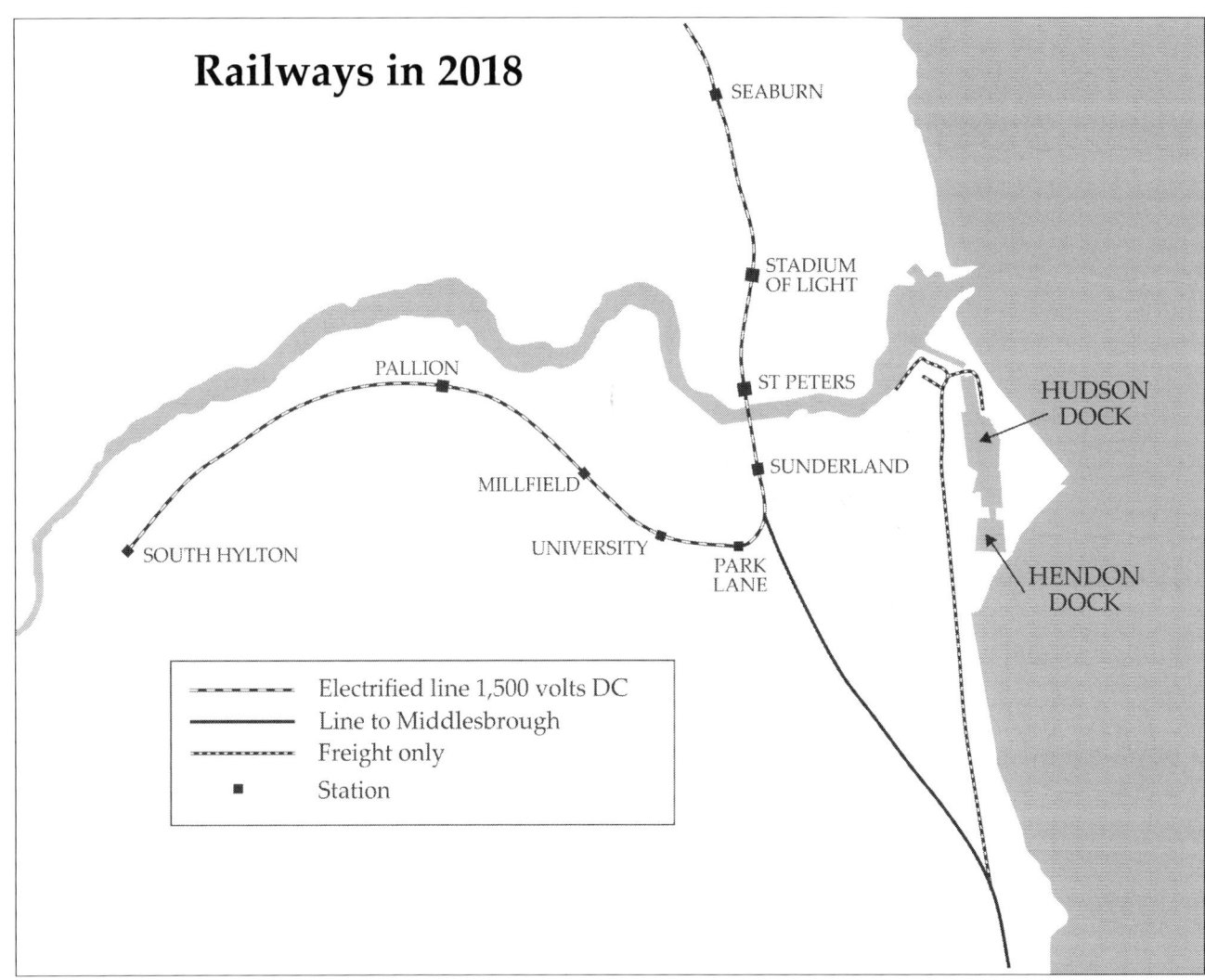

Laying track for Metro extension in Claxheugh cutting, east of South Hylton, in May 2001.

Metrocar at Millfield station on the first day of the Metro service on 31st March, 2002.

Grand Central High Speed Train, headed by class '43' power car No. 43068, passes through Grangetown with a Sunderland to King's Cross service on 3rd March, 2010. These HSTs continued in GC use until the end of 2017 when all services became operated by class 180 diesel multiple units.

since the opening of the Monkwearmouth Junction Railway in 1879.

The initial Metro system was planned by the Tyneside Passenger Transport Authority before Sunderland became part of Tyne and Wear County Council. The fact that the Metro, the first section of which was opened in 1978, did not serve the largest local authority in the County was obviously a source of complaint in Sunderland. A route via Washington was considered for an extension to Sunderland, but it was decided to extend the Metro system over the existing Railtrack line from Pelaw to Sunderland with an extension to South Hylton.

The majority of the construction work for the Metro, which started in 1999, was between Sunderland and South Hylton as the former Penshaw line had been converted to a footpath and cycleway and a new route for the Metro was selected from west of Millfield to west of the former Pallion station. The extension was built as part of the Railtrack network and the route from Pelaw was electrified at the Metro voltage of 1,500V dc.

Metro services began to Sunderland in 2002, operated by the Tyne and Wear Passenger Transport Executive, which had adopted Nexus as it brand name. Additional stations to those at Sunderland and Seaburn were provided within the City boundary at Stadium of Light, St Peter's, Park Lane, University, Millfield, Pallion and South Hylton. The service was operated by the existing Metrocar fleet.

The next major development in Wearside passenger services came in 2007 when 'Open Access' operator Grand Central started a direct service from Sunderland to London via Hartlepool. The Rail Regulator's decision to allow this was challenged by GNER, which was the franchise holder on the East Coast route and lobbied against by the Department of Transport which did not feel that trains to London from the largest city between Leeds and Edinburgh were justified. Nevertheless, the Department included the option of Sunderland to London trains in the East Coast franchise which was won by Virgin Trains in 2015 and one service via Newcastle was introduced. Since 2011 Grand Central has been owned by Sunderland-based Arriva, a subsidiary of Deutsche Bahn.

Privatization has had a negative impact on Sunderland station as it led to division of responsibility between Railtrack and then Network Rail who are responsible for the building and track and the franchise holders who operate Northern trains (one an hour each way) to Middlesbrough through the station. The situation is complicated by the vast majority of trains - the Metro services (five an hour) - being operated by another organization, Nexus and other services being run by Grand Central.

The lack of any sense of 'ownership' of Sunderland by any of the organizations concerned has led to a badly maintained station. It has also meant it is undoubtedly the worst city centre station in the country. Sunderland has been an entirely underground station since the 2000s when Railtrack built over the remaining area of natural light but failed to deliver on upgrading the station. The platform area was rebuilt for used by the Metro and improvements to it, funded by Nexus took place in 2010, but proposals for a major redevelopment, planned in 2012, remained unfulfilled six years later. This is due to the failure of Railtrack's successor, Network Rail, to contribute its promised share of the finance needed.

While in 2018 Sunderland has better services to Newcastle and to London and more stations than ever before, the freight traffic in the area is a shadow of its former self. The traffic for power stations passing through the City includes biomass, now replacing coal, imported at the Tyne Dock Coal terminal and Northumberland opencast coal from North Blyth. There are also cement trains from Dunbar to Seaham and nuclear flask trains from Sellafield to Hartlepool Nuclear Power Station.

Grand Central class '180' diesel multiple unit No. 180105 *The Yorkshire Artist Ashley Jackson* with a terminating train in the Sunderland station on 24th March, 2018. Sunderland will have been the most dismal station it has served since leaving King's Cross.

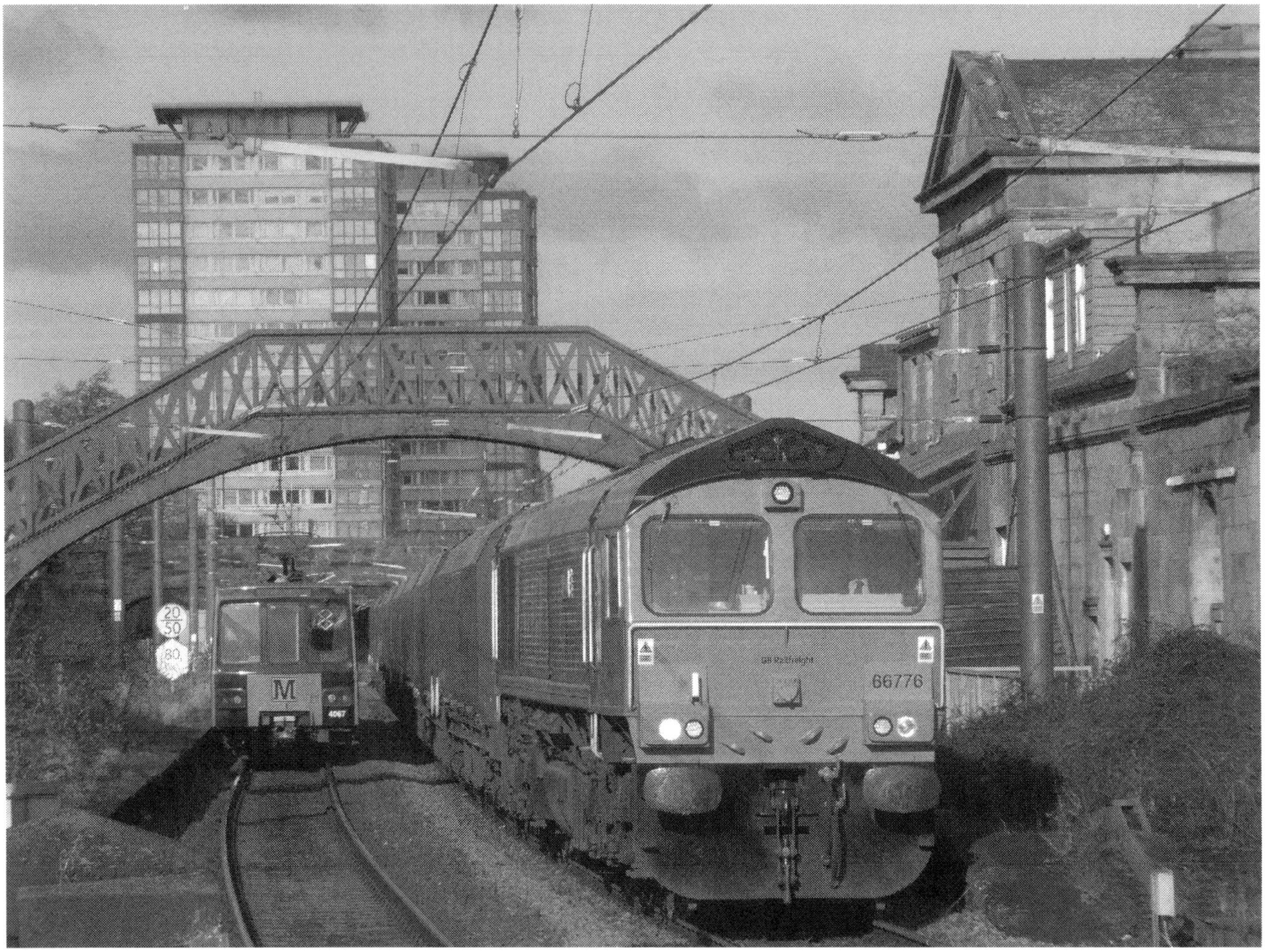

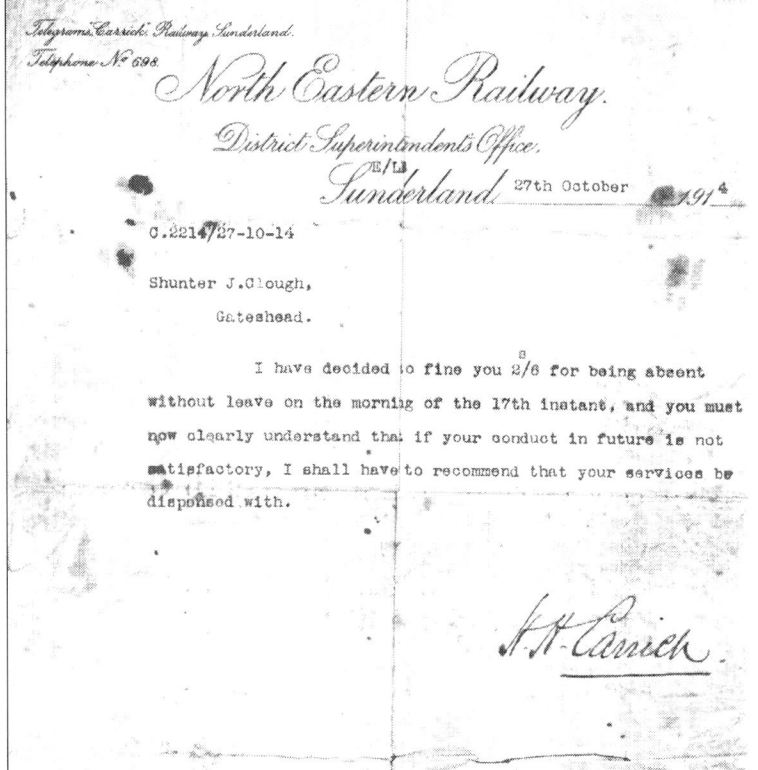

GBRF class '66' No. 66776 *Joanne* with a Tyne Dock to Drax Power Station biomass train passes a Metrocar at Monkwearmouth on 2nd February, 2018.

Telegrams: Carrick: Railway, Sunderland.
Telephone No 698.

North Eastern Railway.

District Superintendent's Office,
E/LB
Sunderland 27th October 1914

C.2214/27-10-14

Shunter J.Clough,
Gateshead.

I have decided to fine you 2/6 for being absent without leave on the morning of the 17th instant, and you must now clearly understand that if your conduct in future is not satisfactory, I shall have to recommend that your services be dispensed with.

Disciplinary letter from the Sunderland District Superintendent in 1914 when his offices were in Hutchinson's Buildings.

The Railway Staff

The railways were a relatively labour-intensive industry and were a significant employer in Sunderland until the 1960s.

The North Eastern Railway had its Sunderland District offices first in Hutchinson's Buildings in High Street West. and then from 1916 in the offices it built in Burdon Road on land it owned at the corner of Burdon Road and Holmeside. Based here were the administrative and clerical staff for the District which extended from Gateshead in the north, Hart in the south and the freight line to Consett in the west.

One of the main centres of railway employment in Sunderland was the South Dock Yard. The yardmaster here was in charge of a team of guards, head shunters, shunters and numbertakers and lamp men who were responsible for the oil lamps fitted on the locomotives and guards' vans. The NER staff were responsible for dealing with the vast number of coal wagons which arrived from the pits and then divided into sets which were shunted onto the staiths for unloading into the colliers. The River Wear Commissioners, who owned the Docks and the staiths, employed the trimmers and teamers who levelled the coal in the colliers. Once the wagons had been emptied they were marshalled into trains and sent back to collieries to be loaded.

The South Dock Yard also housed the NER's main engine shed for the Sunderland area. Its main allocation was locomotives for coal and other freight, although it also housed engines for local passenger services. It was the parent depot for the other main freight sheds in the area at Tyne Dock, Gateshead Borough Gardens and Consett, as well as the shed at Durham.

In charge of the South Dock shed was the shedmaster, who had foremen, fitters and cleaners working for him as well as engine drivers and firemen. Engine drivers were significant members of the community and two, Eden Johnson and William Harvey, became Mayors of Sunderland. Other

NER staff stand in front of '398' class 0-6-0 No. 1406 and a goods train. The locomotive driver and fireman stand on the footplate and the guard, George Carter who was based at South Dock, stands at the front of the engine. The other two are porters or shunters.

William Watson, a North Eastern Railway rolleyman, who collected and delivered goods from Monkwearmouth goods station, photographed in the 1900s.

railwaymen also became councillors, reflecting in part the influence of the National Union of Railwaymen in the local Labour Party. Outside in the yard were a team of wagon examiners and greasers filling the axleboxes of the wagons with grease.

As well as the South Dock yardmaster there was a yardmaster at Monkwearmouth goods station which was officially known as Sunderland goods station. It was the centre for general goods in the town, often delivered by horse-drawn rolleys, and was used by Sunderland industries which did not have their own sidings. Under the Monkwearmouth yardmaster were general, warehouse and yard foremen, shunters, checkers, loaders, goods porters, rolley loaders and cranemen.

Other staff at Monkwearmouth goods station were part of the district goods agent's staff. They included over 50 clerical staff working in the large office where all the paperwork and billing for the traffic was carried out. The district goods agent's staff also included the rolleymen, vanboys, horsemen, trace boys, horsemen and blacksmiths who were based at the nearby stables at Easington Street.

Sunderland Central station had a large number of staff dealing with passengers and parcels and even the smaller stations dealing with both passengers and goods had several workers. Humphrey Household, who was an LNER traffic apprentice at Hylton in 1926, recorded that the staff there were 'a stationmaster, senior clerk, second clerk, two lad porters who worked shifts on the platforms, and a goods porter who worked much of his time at the paper mill sidings...'

Another numerous group of staff were signalmen. At Londonderry and Hendon Junction signal boxes, for instance there were always a signalman on duty throughout the 24-hour period, sometimes with a book lad to record the passage of trains in the register. Also, numerous, but often overlooked, were the members of the civil engineer's department - the

The Monkwearmouth goods station office staff in 1902. Sixth from the left is George Ord, the goods agent for Sunderland. Fourth from the left in the third row from the front is George Dickinson who had started work the previous year at the age of 13 after attending Southwick Board School. There are no women in the photograph, although there was a female cleaner for the offices.

A 1915 photograph of NER workers outside the Monkwearmouth stables in Easington Street. They include the head horsekeeper (centre), rolleymen and farriers. The boys were probably stable lads and trace boys who would have had charge of a second horse when one was needed for heavy loads on rolleys.

David Thompson Hide (1849-1926) and two of his children. He started his railway career at Northallerton before becoming station master at Ryton. He was station master at Monkwearmouth (dealing only with passengers and parcels) from 1882 to 1900 when he moved to Fencehouses from where he retired in 1910.

North Eastern Railway police photographed outside the Monkwearmouth stables about 1915.

A group of Sunderland LNER workers, probably in the mid-1920s. While uniforms were issued to station masters, porters and ticket collectors, this was not the case for clerical staff, such as the booking clerks shown here. The four women shown here reflected the fact number of women employed on the railways had increased from before the 1914 – 1918 War.

Kathy Aisbitt at the gate wheel for the level crossing in Seaton signal box in July 1971. She had previously worked at Springwell and Simonside after training as a signalwoman during the Second World War. After wartime only males were employed in signalling posts and considerable surprise was expressed when Denny Harrison, like Kathy Aisbitt, from a railway family, applied to train in signalling in 1975. She was, nevertheless, appointed to one of the two book lads' positions at Ryhope Grange and became signalwoman at Monkwearmouth.

permanent way squads of gangers and platelayers who inspected and maintained the track. Other NER employees included its police force.

The vast majority of railway employees were male until the latter days of British Railways. In the early years of the 20th century the roles of women had been mainly confined to serving in refreshment rooms or being cleaners. The First World War saw women employed in roles such as porters and clerks in Sunderland. While women continued as clerks after 1918, other roles reverted to being almost exclusively male as servicemen returned from the forces. The same outcome happened after the Second World War when women had carried out a wide range of duties. It was only in the last quarter of the 20th century that the perception of much railway work as being only for men was ended.

Organization of staff continued on broadly similar lines under the LNER and British Railways, latterly under the area manager for Sunderland from 1969 to 1991. There was then a reorganization in the run up to privatization

with Burdon House becoming the office for North East Coal before it was closed. Today the railway staff on Wearside are employed by several different organizations.

The Lambton and Hetton Collieries also had a large number of employees working on their railway. Many carried out similar duties to those in South Dock Yard, but there were also centres of employment at the Hetton (until 1935) and, particularly, the Philadelphia workshops where major repairs and rebuilding of locomotives was carried out. Philadelphia also built locomotives in the 19th century. The town of Sunderland, a major shipbuilding centre, had no locomotive builders, unlike several other North East industrial towns.

With modernization and then reduction in much of the railway traffic on Wearside, there are now far fewer railway workers. But railways still provide employment, albeit of a different type, in that Sunderland is the headquarters of Arriva, which grew out of the motorcycle business of Sir Tom Cowie, near Millfield station. Arriva is now a subsidiary of DB, the German national railway company. It operates trains across seven European countries and buses across 14.

Arriva's headquarters at Doxford Business Park are only a few hundred yards from the route of the Hetton Colliery Railway of 1822. After 200 years railways are still continuing to contribute to the economy of Sunderland, albeit in a very different way.

Left: Pat Gray, area manager for Sunderland from 1969 to 1983. In 1944, like many other staff, he followed his father onto the railways. His first appointment as a station master was in 1952 and he held that position in several stations in Yorkshire and County Durham (including Durham). In his role as area manager he was responsible for both passenger and freight traffic between Pelaw and Billingham.

Right: Arthur Temple whose father and grandfather were the brakesmen at the head of No.3 self-acting incline on the Hetton Railway. After helping his father, unofficially, at the age of eight he started work as a points boy on the Hetton Staiths at 14 in 1949. He then moved to the loco shed at Philadelphia and became a passed fireman and guard and progressing quickly to become an assistant traffic foreman at the age of 25. With declining traffic on the Lambton system, he moved to be surface foreman at Westoe Colliery in South Shields. Arthur Temple's final job was British Coal's manager at the Tyne Dock Coal terminal. In his retirement he was much involved with the development of the Weardale Railway.

A group of NCB Lambton Railway workers outside at Philadelphia in July 1985 just before the closure of the locomotive shed. Left to right are Ronnie Harrison, Phil Merry, Maurice Pitt and Alec Campbell.

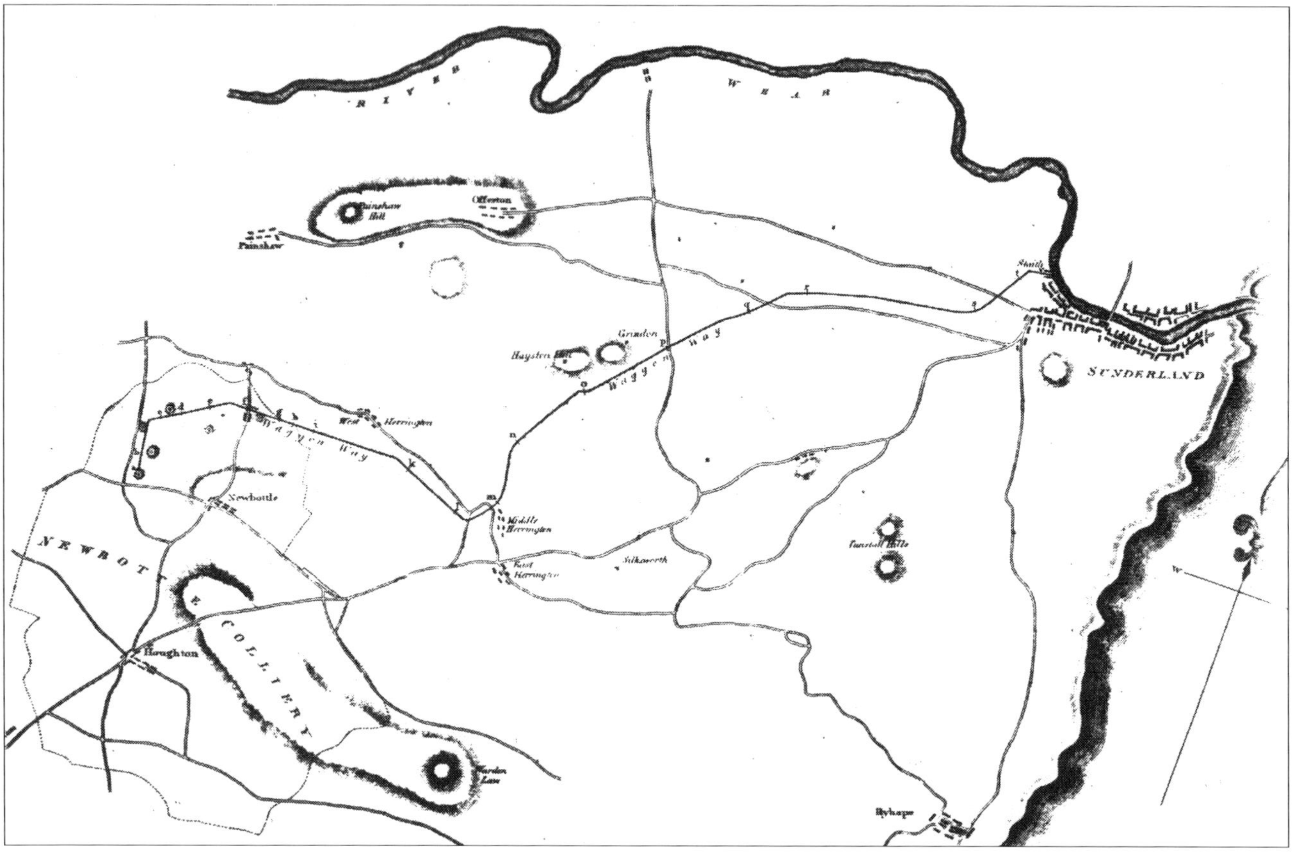

Plan produced for the auction of Nesham's Colliery and Railway in 1822 when John George Lambton was the successful bidder.

Earl of Durham's Railway 0-6-0ST No. 18 (rebuilt by Black, Hawthorn in 1867 from an 0-6-0) at Philadelphia in the 1890s.

Sunderland Railway Lines

The Lambton Railway

At the beginning of the 19th century several of the collieries which were later served by the Lambton system, such as Lambton, Lumley, Newbottle, Harraton and North Biddick pits, were connected by wagonways to the Wear west of Cox Green.

In 1812 the Nesham family abandoned their earlier staiths in favour of a new railway from Newbottle colliery to staiths below the Sunderland iron bridge. This was operated by horses with a self-acting incline to the new staiths. In 1822 this line was purchased at auction by John George Lambton, later the 1st Earl of Durham, who linked it to the Lambton and Lumley wagonways. After 1822 much of the horse working was replaced by stationary engines and self-acting inclines. In the early 1830s the Newbottle route (now also carrying coal from the pits developed by Lambton from Fence Houses to Sherburn) was replaced between Philadelphia and Grindon.

Lambton Railway locomotives and wagons started to use the NER's Penshaw branch from the mid-1850s when a link was built from Millfield to the existing line at Hylton Road (*see map page 8*). A new route to the Lambton Staiths was created in 1865 by building a line, through a tunnel, from the NER's short Deptford line off the Penshaw branch. Running powers for Lambton trains were also secured to the Hudson Dock and from Harraton Colliery to Penshaw. Most of the old route was then abandoned.

For much of the second half of the 19th century the line was known as the Earl of Durham's Railway, but in 1895 the 3rd Earl sold his collieries and

The Lambton Engine Works yard at Philadelphia in 1891. This was the centre of the Lambton Collieries engineering operations. The locomotive repair shop overhauled and indeed built, engines. There was also a boiler shop, fitting shop, foundries, rolling mills wagon shops as well as the main Lambton engine sheds.

railway to Sir James Joicey. The Lambton Railway ceased operation south of Fencehouses on 1st January, 1914 when the Sherburn Collieries were sold.

Joicey's coal interests expanded when Lambton Collieries Company took over the Hetton Coal and North Hetton Coal Companies in 1911. After a further merger with the original Joicey collieries the company became the Lambton, Hetton and Joicey Collieries Ltd. The Joicey system in the Beamish area remained distinct from the Lambton and Hetton system. In 1947 all the collieries passed to the National Coal Board.

The major contraction of the Lambton system began in the 1960s with the closure of several collieries and NCB working over the Penshaw branch ceased in 1967. The line to Houghton closed in 1975, that to Philadelphia Works and Herrington Colliery in 1984 and the final section to Lambton Coke Works in 1986.

NCB 0-6-0ST No. 51 (Robert Stephenson & Hawthorns, 1944) passes Philadelphia with a coal train from Herrington Colliery in 1968. The Lambton Engine Works can be seen on the right.

NCB No. 5 (Robert Stephenson, 1909) under repair in the works at Philadelphia on 17th July, 1968. This engine is now preserved on the North Yorkshire Moors Railway.

Lambton Railway 0-6-0 No. 25 (Lambton Engine Works, 1890) at Philadelphia in the 1930s. The lower of the two sets of buffers was for chaldron wagons.

NCB, former British Railways diesel-hydraulic 0-6-0s built at Swindon in 1965, No. D9540 and No. D9525, stand along the coaling gantry at Philadelphia on 15th February, 1969. The acquisition of these locomotives led to the withdrawal of the last steam engines on the Lambton system.

0-4-0 electric locomotive (Robert Stephenson & Hawthorns, 1954) at the Lambton Coke Works at Fencehouses on 12th August, 1970. It is about to propel its coking car from the ovens a few yards along the rack to the quenching tower.

NCB 0-6-0DE No. 513 (formerly BR No. 12098) shunts wagons at Lambton Coke Works on 2nd June, 1985, seven months before the closure of the Coke Works and the final section of the Lambton Railway to Penshaw Yard.

NCB 0-6-2 No. 31 (Kitson,1907) passes Burnmoor Crossing with coal wagons for Penshaw Yard on 25th August, 1967.

NCB 0-6-0DE No. 510 (former BR No. 12120) at Carter's Coal Depot at Penshaw on its final day of operation on 23rd August, 1973. The uneven state of the track leading up to the coal drops is apparent.

NCB 0-6-2T No. 42 (Robert Stephenson, 1920) at Penshaw North with coal empties from Sunderland for Harraton Colliery on 26th August, 1964. The NCB brake van is next to the engine after the engine had run round following its arrival from Sunderland over the NCB lines on the right. The train will reverse again at Washington before reaching Harraton. The bridge abutments to the right of the NER overhead signal box carried the Lambton wagonway down to Low Lambton Staiths.

The 1830s course of the Lambton wagonway can be seen running from the bottom right past the house of Grindon Close (later a library and museum). The pond in the grounds was originally the water supply for the second Grindon stationary engine. The route of Nesham's 1812 line can be seen coming in in the middle right of the photograph which was probably taken in the late 1930s. Just beyond the point where the two routes joined, all traces disappear. It continued over Chester Road through the trees of Bishopwearmouth Cemetery in the top left. Post-war building led to the loss of all traces of the wagonways.

Lambton Railway bridge at the Chester Road (Farnham Terrace) entrance to Bishopwearmouth Cemetery which was built about 1855. The photograph was taken in 1965 shortly before the bridge was demolished and the cemetery entrance levelled.

Once claimed to be 'the oldest working locomotive in the world' when it was withdrawn in 1909, the date of the building of this Hetton Colliery 0-4-0 is now believed to be 1852, not 1822. It was rebuilt in 1871. The engine was preserved after taking part in the Stockton and Darlington Railway Centenary Celebrations in 1925.

The former Hetton Colliery Railway Locomotive Fitting Shop at Hetton Lyons in 1978.

The Hetton Colliery Railway

The line was opened in 1822 from Hetton Lyons Colliery to the staiths at Sunderland, with later branches to Eppleton and Elemore Collieries. By the late 1850s the Hetton Coal Company also controlled the North Hetton Coal Company with its Hazard and Moorsley Collieries. The coal from these pits went out over the Londonderry Railway until it was closed west of Seaham in 1896. The North Hetton pits were then linked to the Hetton line at the Copt Hill incline.

After both the Hetton and North Hetton companies were acquired by Sir James Joicey, a link was made in 1916 to the Lambton system near Rainton Meadows. Part of this line closed with Moorsley Colliery in 1935, but the remainder of the branch was retained until the late 1950s for used by colliery locomotives travelling from Hetton to Philadelphia via the LNER/BR line and North Hetton junction.

The route between Silksworth Lane and Hetton Staiths in Sunderland was realigned in different stages between about 1890 and 1910 and a link was constructed to Silksworth Colliery after Joicey purchased it from the Londonderry Collieries in 1920.

Hetton Lyons Colliery closed in 1950. After the opening of Hawthorn Combined Mine in Murton in 1959, coal ceased to be drawn up at Elemore and Eppleton and the line was closed south of Silksworth Colliery Junction. The Railway closed in 1967 from Hylton Road to the Staiths and in 1972 from Silksworth Colliery to Hylton Road Coal Depot. Much of the route is now a footpath and cycleway – the Stephenson Trail.

NCB 0-4-0ST No. 13 (Hawthorn, Leslie, 1914) crossing Caroline Street in Hetton-le-Hole returning from Hetton Dene to the locomotive sheds at Hetton Lyons on 19th August, 1959. The Lyons Colliery had closed in 1950, but the shed remained open to serve the lines to Elemore and Eppleton Collieries.

NCB 0-6-0T No. 41 (Kerr, Stuart, 1917) at the Three Tuns crossing on the relatively level section in Hetton Dene on 27th August 1959, returning from taking coal wagons to the bottom of Copt Hill incline. All the photographs showing the line a few weeks before the closure of the majority of the Hetton Railway on 9th September, 1959 were taken by Ian Carr. Here, as elsewhere on Wearside, he photographed scenes which would otherwise have been unrecorded.

Copt Hill Engine House on 26th August, 1959 looking towards the summit of the line at Warden Law (about 600 feet above sea level) whose stationary engine house can be seen in the distance above the wagons on the right.

The foot of No.1/the top of No.2 incline between Warden Law and North Moor in August 1959. On the left the rope is being attached for the full wagons to descend. The full wagons pulled up the empty wagons returning from the staiths.

Renewal of the bridge over the road leading from Silksworth to East Herrington, probably in the 1900s.

NCB 0-6-0ST No. 58 (Vulcan Foundry, 1945) at Plains Farm in August 1959 with a coal train, which it had taken over at the foot of the No.4 Incline at North Moor.

0-4-0ST No. 43 (Grant Ritchie, 1920) running light to Silksworth Colliery on 25th March, 1957. It is on the connecting line from the colliery to the Hetton Colliery Railway which is parallel on the higher level behind; the Silksworth line is about to join the HCR. Humbledon Hill is in the background.

NCB 0-6-0DE No. 514 (former British Railways 12084) emerges from the tunnel under Durham Road at the Barnes on 1st June, 1972, the HCR's final month of operation as the headboard denotes. The tunnel replaced two level crossings. The empty coal wagons were being taken from the Railway Row Coal Depot to Silksworth Colliery, where they were handed over to British Railways diesel locomotives.

An HCR 0-6-0ST, probably No. 4, crosses Durham Road with an empty coal train in the 1890s/early 1900s. The house on the left is in Ivanhoe Crescent. This route was replaced by the Barnes tunnel.

HCR 0-6-0ST No. 8 (R&W Hawthorn, 1870) outside the Hetton Colliery Railway Sunderland shed in Durham Road (later the site of the Mayfair building). It was demolished in the 1920s after its locomotives were transferred to a new shed at the Lambton Staiths.

The Lambton and Hetton Staiths

The Newbottle (later Lambton) Staiths were opened in 1812 and the Hetton Staiths in 1822; the railway inclines to both were opened by self-acting inclines. The Hetton Colliery Railway added a further incline worked by a stationary engine.

The Lambton incline was replaced by the Deptford Tunnel in 1865 and the Hetton Colliery incline by a tunnel under Hylton Road about 1890. A link, by tunnel, was put in between the Lambton and Hetton Staiths in the 1910s. The Hetton Staiths closed in 1962 and the Lambton Staiths and approach lines closed in 1967.

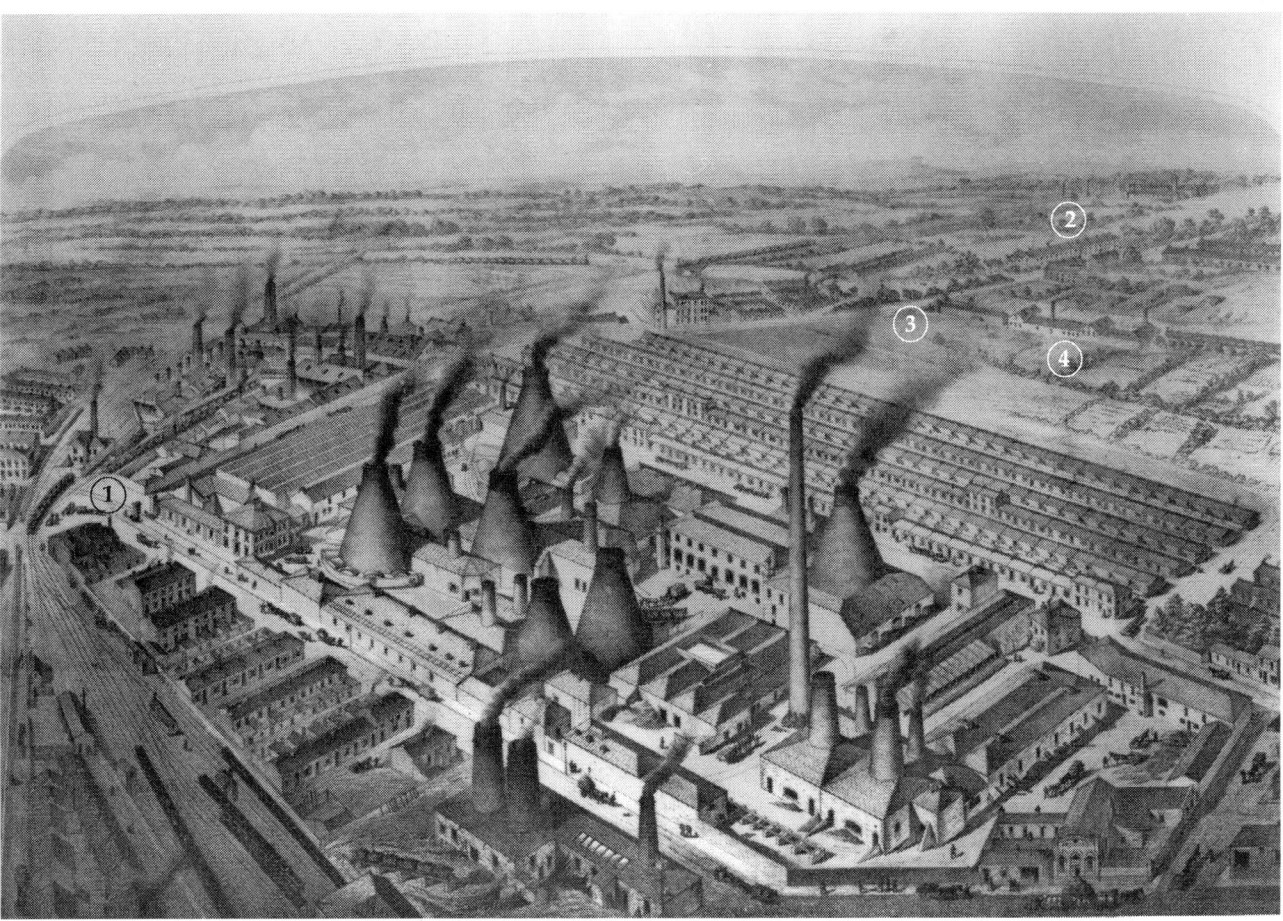

A print produced about 1855 showing Hartley's glassworks which, at the time, was said to have produced one-third of all the plate glass produced in Britain (including for stations such as Monkwearmouth and Paddington). One of the reasons why James Hartley, later a Director of the NER, located his works in 1833 at the junction of Hylton Road and Trimdon Street was because coal for his furnaces could come in by the Hetton Colliery Railway. This line can be seen coming into the left of the HCR stationary engine house (1). The Lambton Collieries Railway comes in past its Glebe Engine (2) near the present Sunderland Royal Hospital to cross the Hetton line. The Penshaw line of the NER passes Millfield station (3) and Burlinson's Millfield Engine Works (4) which in 1856 repaired Londonderry Railway locomotives.

NCB 0-4-0DH No. 157 (Hunslet, 1967) returns from the coal depot at Railway Row on 6th August, 1970 with empty wagons to be handed over to a BR locomotive at Silksworth Colliery. The disused line on the left dropped down to the tunnel under Hylton Road and then to the Hetton Staiths. The chimney of the electricity works can be seen in the background.

Newbottle Railway plan of 1817. The building marked 'Staiths' is a landsale (coal depot). The first staiths in the area (then known as drops) are the served by the line running at right angles to the depot close to gardens of Bishopwearmouth Rectory.

Aerial view of the Lambton and Hetton Staiths about 1928. On the south bank of the Wear, in the bottom left, are the low-level Hetton Staiths which had probably ceased to be used. Above them are the two high-level Hetton Staiths. The area almost up to the NER bridge is occupied by the Lambton Staiths.

Lambton Railway 0-6-0 No. 20 (Robert Stephenson, 1876) at the Staiths about 1900. The Railway's earliest 0-6-0 tender engines were purchased in 1852-4 and worked to the top of the Staiths incline by the link from Millfield on the Penshaw branch probably opened in 1853. From 1865 Lambton coal trains reached the staiths by the tunnel from the new Deptford branch.

View of Lambton Staiths from the footplate of an NCB 0-6-2T in 1965. The 1879 railway bridge and the 1929 road bridge can be seen in the background.

NCB 0-4-0ST No. 39 (Robert Stephenson & Hawthorns, 1953) takes water outside the engine shed at Lambton Staiths on 26th August, 1964. 0-4-0ST No. 35 (Hawthorn, Leslie, 1913) shunts on the right. The left-hand tunnel was the Lambton line to Deptford Junction, while the right-hand was the connection to the Hetton Staiths built in the 1910s. The restrictions of the Lambton tunnel were the reason for the system's locomotives having rounded or tapered cabs.

The Brandling Junction Railway

The BJR opened in 1839 with services from both Gateshead and South Shields to Wearmouth station and a freight only branch to the North Dock. In 1848 Monkwearmouth station replaced Wearmouth, which then became solely used for freight. In the same year, with the opening of the High Level Bridge over the Tyne, the train service was extended to Newcastle.

The line became part of the route to the south after the opening of the Monkwearmouth Junction line in 1879. Seaburn station was opened in 1937. The lower part of the North Dock, reached by a rope-worked incline, powered first by a stationary steam engine and then by an electric winder, closed in the 1950s. The upper section closed in the mid-1960s. The Sunderland to South Shields passenger service was withdrawn in 1965 and Monkwearmouth station closed to passengers in 1967.

The line was electrified and became part of the Tyne and Wear Metro system in 2002 with new stations at the Stadium of Light and St Peter's.

'A8' class 4-6-2 No. 69871 heads a Sunderland to Newcastle train between Seaburn and East Boldon stations on 31st January, 1954, having crossed the Sunderland municipal boundary.

Sir Hedworth Williamson's Limeworks *Sylvia* (Hudswell, Clarke, 1927) in 1956 at the exchange sidings with BR north of Seaburn station. The Fulwell Limeworks produced a significant amount of outward railway traffic. In the early 1920 it was 90,000 tons a year. Closure took place in 1957 with the company continuing production of lime at its other quarry at Kirkby Stephen.

One of Sir Hedworth Williamson's Hudswell, Clarke 0-4-0STs propelling wagons of limestone onto the Spencer kilns at Fulwell. The kilns produce hydrate lime which was discharged into wagons at the bottom.

Metro-Cammell diesel multiple unit at Seaburn station in the mid-1960s. This station opened in 1937 to serve Sunderland's growing suburbs in the Fulwell area and its seaside resort at Seaburn. It also replaced the football platform in Forfar Street as the station for Roker Park ground. In this view the southbound platform has acquired a North Eastern Railway seat with 'snake' supports. The main station buildings were situated at the top of the ramp behind and were rebuilt in 1953. The station was rebuilt again, with lifts, for the introduction of the Metro service.

'J27' class 0-6-0 No. 65887 runs round its train at Fulwell Road Crossing in 1963, having brought coal wagons to Crowder's coal depot. The sidings here were also used to store carriages. Since the 1950s this had been the end of the North Dock branch. In the left background a double-deck bus can be seen at Sunderland Corporation Transport's Fulwell Depot.

Sunderland's Railways

LNER 'B17' 4-6-0 No. 2854 *Sunderland* after being named after the town's football club by the chairman Sir Walter Raine (fourth from left under nameplate) on sidings on the North Dock branch close to the Roker Park ground in April 1936.

The North Dock on 22nd April, 1982. Engineered by Isambard Kingdom Brunel (1806-1859), it was opened in 1837 and linked to the Brandling Junction Railway two years later. It was purchased by George Hudson's York, Newcastle and Berwick Railway in 1846, but was never a commercial success and was soon completely overshadowed by the South Docks. Ownership passed to the River Wear Commissioners in 1922. By the 1890s the North Dock was used for timber traffic by the North Eastern Railway and Armstrong Addison who produced many of the NER's sleepers and timber bridge baulks. Although isolated from the main railway system after the 1950s, the firm operated on the site until 1990. It retained railway track used by its steam cranes which can be seen, along with Scotch derricks in this view. The dock is now a marina surrounded by housing.

Class '47' No. 1859 passes Wearmouth Junction signal box with a Newcastle to Liverpool train in April 1973. The course of the line to goods yard in Portobello Lane, where the BJR's Wearmouth station was situated, can be seen to the right of the locomotive. The yard served coal depots, Wilson's timber yard and Tyzack's foundry.

A Metrocar pauses at the Stadium of Light station on 24th January, 2017. The station takes its name from the nearby ground of Sunderland Football Club. The availability of the trackbed of the former extensive lines in this area has provided space for a car park and the ramps to the southbound platform.

Monkwearmouth station in the 1900s. The roof of the passenger station can be seen above the screen walls; this was removed in 1928. The roof of the goods station is beyond.

'4MT' class 2-6-0 No. 76021 approaches Monkwearmouth station with a return excursion train on 11th August, 1962. The '03' 0-6-0DM shunting wagons is acting as the Monkwearmouth area pilot for the goods yard and the other goods facilities in the area. The goods station was the main centre for freight, other than coal, in Sunderland. The shed was extended in the 1870s, 1890s and 1900s. In addition to receiving many types of goods for distribution in the town there was outward traffic from local industries, including ropes and beer.

Monkwearmouth in 1976. From the left are preserved rolling stock in the re-laid loading dock area, Monkwearmouth Station Museum with its platform gallery, the restored 1879 footbridge and waiting shelter and the goods shed and yard. From 1973 to 2017 Monkwearmouth station was a museum of land transport. It then became the Fans Museum devoted to Sunderland Football Club. In this photograph the goods yard is being used for unloading steel for the shipyards. A steam rail mounted crane once operated on track in front of the National Carriers (NCL) trailer.

Class '47' No. 47853 (repainted in the unique XP64 livery it carried as No. D1733 in 1964) passes the former Monkwearmouth station on 11th June, 2008 with a diverted Grand Central York to Sunderland service arriving from the north. At this stage Grand Central were only operating a service between York and Sunderland with a locomotive on either end. Due to the earlier failure of No. 47839 at the rear, the train had travelled via Durham so that No. 47853 could work the return train south from Sunderland by the usual route via Hartlepool.

The stables for Monkwearmouth goods station which were built 1884 in Easington Street. They had 100 stalls plus looseboxes, a hayloft and stalls, a blacksmith's shop, a mess hall for the workers and two houses for the staff. The building later became a garage for railway delivery vehicles. Photographed on 20th June, 1988, it still survives in 2018.

St Peter's Metro station in April 2018. It is built on the approaches to Wearmouth bridge and close to Monkwearmouth station, both listed structures. The station was designed not to detract from these. To acknowledge Sunderland's history of glassmaking, which began in the nearby St Peter's Anglo-Saxon Church and continues in the National Glass Centre, the shelters, including the platform under them, and the lift towers were constructed of glass. The station serves the St Peter's campus of Sunderland University.

The Monkwearmouth Junction Railway

The line was opened from Monkwearmouth station to Ryhope Grange Junction in 1879, linking the North Eastern Railway's systems on the north and south banks of the Wear. The main features were the bridge across the Wear, a central station and the tunnels north and south of the station. The station's official name has always been Sunderland, although it has usually been known locally as the Central station.

The route was electrified as far as the junction with the Penshaw branch, at the south end of Sunderland station, when it became part of the Tyne and Wear Metro system in 2002.

Direct Rail Services class '20' No. 20312 and 20311 crossed the Wearmouth Bridge with a flask from Sellafield to Hartlepool Nuclear Power Station on 27th January, 1999.

William Bell's revised plans for Sunderland station. The original design had been heavily criticized in the local press as being not equal to stations with smaller populations like South Shields or Durham 'even to that of Ferryhill'. A deputation of Councillors met the NER Directors in Newcastle and the High Street West frontage was altered and a Gothic clocktower added.

Sunderland Corporation tram No. 74 passes the High Street West (the North end) entrance of the station in the early 1950s; Sunderland trams ceased in 1954. A glazed canopy for horse-drawn cabs was built in 1897. In 1938 the shops shown here were built under the canopy between the pavement and the taxi rank. The LNER's logos on either side of the Sunderland station sign have been removed after nationalization.

The interior of the North end of Sunderland station on 7th June, 1964 looking towards High Street West. The North end, the main entrance to the station which many people recalled as 'always smelling of fish' was demolished in 1966 and Littlewoods Store was built on its site.

The station in 1938 showing the ramps to the entrance at the South end. This had its own ticket office and tickets issued at the two entrances were distinguished by the letters 'N' and 'S'. The overall roof was designed by Thomas Harrison.

'G5' 0-4-4T No. 67253 with a Sunderland to South Shields train on 29th April, 1958, looking to the South end. The canopies were first erected in the area made roofless by the 1941 bomb and then extended in 1952-3 when the remainder of the overall roof was removed during the first modernization of the station. All passenger services were concentrated on the East (left-hand side) island platform after remodelling of the layout in 1965 following withdrawal of local services to Durham, South Shields and West Hartlepool. The other platform was then used for parcels.

'V1' class 2-6-2T No. 67677 pulls out of Sunderland on 14th September, 1957. Sunderland signal box is on the left. In the background is the second South entrance which opened in 1953 and the tower at the North end, partly obscured by steam.

The South entrance to the station which became the main entrance after it was rebuilt in 1965. When this photograph was taken on 22nd February, 1976 it still possessed facilities such as toilets and a bookstall, which have now vanished. In 2018 the building is extremely run down, with one of the two destination and arrival indicators on the concourse having been out of action for 10 years.

'Pacer' No. 143020, one of six in Tyne and Wear Passenger Transport Executive yellow and white livery, which was also applied to Metrocars and many buses in the County before deregulation in October 1986, two months after this photograph was taken on 14th August. Although the north end of the station had been built over the passenger experience on the platform area was still relatively pleasant with natural light and hanging baskets for flowers. Sunderland station always suffered from being in a cutting below ground level, but it was only the complete removal of natural light by construction of shops over the platforms in the south end and then the centre that has made it so depressing.

The platform area at Sunderland looking north on 8th April, 2018 showing the single, widened island platform. Northern trains stop at the north end and Metrocars at the south. The loss of natural light is only partly offset by the illuminated wall with moving figures to the west of the platform.

The new North entrance to the station on 23rd June, 2018. This must be the least impressive entrance to any station in Britain, let alone to one from the main shopping area of the largest city between Leeds and Edinburgh.

'Peak' No. 45023 *The Royal Pioneer Corps* emerges from Sunderland South Tunnel with the Summer Saturday Scarborough to Newcastle train on 9th June, 1984, the final year of the operation of this, the last regular locomotive-hauled train through Sunderland. A Metro-Cammell two-car dmu, with a Tyne and Wear PTE logo, waits to leave the sidings to take up a Sunderland to Newcastle working. Between the trains is Sunderland signal box which controlled the colour light signalling installed in 1965 until 2002 when control of the signals on the line to Newcastle were transferred to the Tyneside Integrated Electronic Control Centre in Gateshead.

'V2' 2-6-2 No. 60843, with an empty stock train, passes Vilette Road signal box in the early 1960s.

A Durham Miners' Gala Day scene at Hetton, the most westerly of the D&SR stations within the Sunderland boundaries, in July 1950. The driver of a 'J39' class 0-6-0 is exchanging single line tokens before entering the station. The train is bound for Durham Elvet stations close to the Gala proceedings. The line beyond Pittington to Durham Elvet had been closed to normal passenger services in 1931. The goods shed is on the left and the Hetton Colliery Railway crosses in the background.

'J39' 0-6-0 No. 64947 collects the single line token for Hetton at Murton on the line to Durham Elvet station for the Miners' Gala in the early 1950s. To the right of the signal box is the line to Haswell and Hartlepool.

The Durham and Sunderland and Londonderry Railways

The Durham and Sunderland Railway opened in 1836 from staiths on the River Wear and a passenger station on the Town Moor, first to Haswell and then from Murton Junction via Hetton to Pitttington with an extension to Shincliffe being completed in 1839. The line to the staiths was abandoned after the opening of the South Dock in 1850.

The Londonderry Railway (Seaham and Sunderland Section) carried freight to the South Dock from 1854 and passengers to Hendon Burn station from 1855. A branch was built to Ryhope Colliery in 1859 and extended to Silksworth Colliery in 1871.

In 1858 the Town Moor was replaced by Hendon station which also served Londonderry passenger trains from 1868. Hendon closed on the opening of the Monkwearmouth Junction line with its new central station and the lines north of Ryhope Grange Junction then became freight only.

Durham Elvet replaced Shincliffe as the terminus of the line via Hetton in 1893. Passenger services on the Durham and Sunderland route between Pittington and Elvet ceased in 1931 and between Sunderland and Pittington in 1953. Ryhope East station closed in 1960 and the branch to Silksworth in 1972. The final section of the Durham and Sunderland closed in 1993. The Londonderry line from Ryhope Grange remains in use as part of the Newcastle to Middlesbrough route.

'G5' class 0-4-4T No. 67267 pilots an 'A1' class 4-6-2 up the bank at Seaton with a train diverted via Haswell from the line via Seaham due to engineering work in the mid-1950s. In the background, to the right of the train, is Seaton station.

'J27' class 0-6-0 No. 65812 heads a coal train down Seaton Bank in the 1950s. The station building on the right building dates from the 1850s when Seaton station was resited from its original site almost a mile north after the Durham and Sunderland was converted from rope to locomotive working. The similar station building at Hetton was probably also built after conversion to locomotive working.

'V3' class 2-6-2T No. 67687 and 'A3' class 4-6-2 No. 60050 *Persimmon* storm away from Ryhope on the 1 in 55 gradient stretch of Seaton Bank on 28th May, 1961 with a diverted Newcastle to King's Cross train. Because of the steepness of Seaton Bank, as much as 1 in 42 at one point (due to the Durham and Sunderland originally being designed for rope working by stationary engines), southbound diverted expresses were often assisted by a second locomotive from Sunderland to Haswell.

A pair of NER class '398' 0-6-0s with the breakdown train at Ryhope after the accident in 1889 when a Liverpool to Newcastle train had come down the steep bank and derailed on a sharp curve at the bottom. 101 passengers were injured. The carts in the foreground are waiting at the level crossing in Robson Place. The original Ryhope station on the Durham and Sunderland line was to the left.

The second Ryhope station built in 1894 after the NER realigned the curve as a result of the 1889 derailment. The Sunderland to Stockton road was diverted under the railway. The position of the Robson Place level crossing is marked by the footbridge.

'L1' 2-6-4T No. 67755 heads a Newcastle to Middlesbrough train past Ryhope on 28th August, 1957. The first Londonderry station at Ryhope was probably a platform near the grassed area behind the brick building in the foreground, with the Durham and Sunderland station site being to its left out of this view.

The second Londonderry Ryhope station. Designed by Brewer, the Marquis of Londonderry's Estate Clerk of Works, the station and the footbridge were markedly different from NER stations. East was added to the satation name in 1904 after the North Eastern's acquisition of the Londonderry line to Seaham.

Grand Central High Speed Train headed by class '43' power car No. 43468 on a Sunderland to King's Cross service passing the boundary of the City at Ryhope Dene on 30th June, 2014. These units were used on services to London from 2007 to 2017. The High Speed Trains were previously used through Sunderland on British Rail's *Cleveland Executive* and, since 2016, on the one service from the City to London via Newcastle.

Class 'Q6' 0-8-0 No. 63458 with brake van crosses the bridge marked 'LS&SR' (Londonderry Seaham and Sunderland Railway, over the lane to Ryhope beach on its way to Seaham on 28th October, 1966.

'Deltic' No. D9005 *The Prince of Wales Own Regiment of Yorkshire* approaching Ryhope with the Sunday-only Newcastle to King's Cross via Sunderland train on the Londonderry line on 5th November 1972. The track curving off to the left over the Durham and Sunderland line is the disused line to Ryhope and Silksworth Collieries.

'J27' class 0-6-0 No. 65865 with a coal train from Silksworth approaching Ryhope Colliery in October 1966. St Paul's Church is in the left background.

'J27' 0-6-0 No. 65879 climbs from Ryhope to Silksworth Colliery with empty coal wagons in August 1967. The line from Ryhope was extended to Silksworth when the Marquis of Londonderry opened the pit in 1871. The Londonderry Collieries retained ownership of the Ryhope to Silksworth section after the Seaham and Sunderland Railway was sold in 1900, but it was worked by the NER and its successors.

'J27' 0-6-0 No. 65894 at Silksworth Colliery in August 1967.

NCB 0-4-0ST No. 47 (Stephenson and Hawthorns, 1923) shunts at Silksworth Colliery on 25th March, 1957.

Silksworth Colliery on 5th August, 1967 with class '03' No. D2074 and No. D2071 on the branch from Ryhope (*right*) and NCB 0-4-0DH 157 (Hunslet, 1967) on the link from the Hetton Colliery Railway (*left*). The NCB locomotive will take the wagons down to coal depots in Sunderland. Both lines to Silksworth closed when this traffic ceased in June 1972. No. D2074 and No. D2071, were dreen liveried locomotive which had been converted to work in multiple on the Silksworth line and were known locally as 'Pixie and Dixie' No. D2052 and No. D2053, blue liveried '03's, which had also been converted to work in multiple, were known as 'Pinky and Perky'. The nicknames came from popular cartoon characters of the period.

Colas Rail Freight class '60' No. 60085 approaching Ryhope Grange with a train of Seaham to Oxwellmains (Dunbar) empty cement wagons on 4th May, 2016. The former Durham and Sunderland lines and the Ryhope Grange sidings are on the right.

Class '47' No. D1810 with a 29 vehicle parcels special from sidings by the Brian Mills Depot (seen on the left) to Gloucester on 26th July, 1969. The mail order depot generated much parcels traffic during the late 1960s and early 1970s with, at one time, four trains leaving Sunderland most evenings. The traffic ceased in 1981. The Durham and Sunderland and Londonderry lines ran parallel from Ryhope to Hendon Junction.

Direct Rail Services class '37' Nos. 37607 and 37609 top and tail a Network Rail track recording train on 8th May, 2014 past Ryhope Grange signal box. This is the last signal box on Wearside and controls the colour light signals on the Durham Coast line as far as Seaton Carew, south of Hartlepool. The then-disused line to the South Docks can be seen curving away to the right opposite the signal box.

Class '66' No. 66755 (with 66735 at the rear of the carriages) heads the 'Tale of Two Ports' railtour back to Ryhope Grange Junction on 29th August 2016, 18 months after the line to the South Docks had been reopened. The docks can be seen in the right background.

The former Hendon station in the 1960s. This was the terminus of trains on the former Durham and Sunderland line from 1858 and Londonderry trains from 1868 to 1879. It was afterwards converted to a Mineral Office and was latterly used by the South Dock yardmaster. The left-hand section was added in the 1900s. The Penshaw branch ran behind the building.

Class '56' No. 56077 on the Penshaw branch at Hendon Junction on 23rd July, 1984. Leaning out of the cab door is Bob Blackburn, a well-known Sunderland driver. On the left is Hendon Junction signal box which was destroyed by fire in 1995.

The South Docks

The Durham and Sunderland was the first railway in this area when it was opened to the carry both passengers and goods to the station on the Town Moor and coal to staiths on the Low Quay. The opening of the South Dock in 1850 led to the closure of the staiths. The Town Moor station closed in 1858 as the tracks leading to it were needed for increasing coal traffic for shipment. In 1859 the South Dock Company sold out to the River Wear Commissioners who added the Hendon Dock as a southern extension in 1868. The original dock became known as the Hudson Dock and the complex as the South Docks, although the North Eastern Railway continued to refer to South Dock in the singular for its extensive sidings, goods station and engine shed in the area.

The staiths, and later conveyor belts, in the Docks were owned by the River Wear Commissioners, but all traffic to these was worked by the North Eastern Railway and its successors. The River Wear Commissioners were replaced by the Port of Sunderland Authority in 1972. Rail traffic ceased in the early 2000s, but the connection to the national network was restored in 2015.

This aerial view taken in the 1920s or 1930s shows the Hudson Dock, with its staiths, on the left and the Hendon Dock on the right. It also shows the many sidings of the LNER to the left of the Docks.

The Station Hotel in Prospect Row on 22nd May, 1965 with Sunderland Corporation bus 41 on the Docks service. The Hotel was named after the Town Moor station which had closed 107 years earlier! To the right is St John's Church with, in the distance, the Prospect public house which has survived the demolition of much of the area.

The first type of staith to be used at the South Docks. The chaldron wagons were lowered down to the collier ships. In later staiths coal was delivered through spouts and then electrically powered conveyor belts were introduced.

SUNDERLAND RAILWAY LINES: THE SOUTH DOCKS

This view taken from the brake van of a railtour on 15th May, 1965 shows the sidings leading to the staiths on either side of 'WD' 2-8-0 No. 90445 with the conveyor belts in the distance to the right of the locomotive. To its left are St John's Church and the coaling stage for South Dock Depot.

Four class 'J27' 0-6-0s gather around the turntable in South Dock Shed in September 1967. The roundhouse was built in 1875. There was also a two-road straight shed which appears to be an earlier structure. This was rebuilt by British Railways and continued to house diesels after the end of steam traction.

'WD' 2-8-0 No. 90417, 'Q6' 0-8-0 No. 63395, '08' 0-6-0DE No. D3943 and 'J27' 0-6-0 No. 65894 outside South Dock Motive Power Depot on 9th September, 1967, just before the shed closed to steam. The 'Q6's and the 'J27's were the last pre-grouping locomotives on British Railways. Both No. 63395 and No. 65894 were purchased and restored by the North Eastern Locomotive Preservation Group and are now on the North Yorkshire Moors Railway. The 2-8-0s were too large to turn in the roundhouse and for this purpose had to use the triangle of lines Tile Shed – Harton Junction – Brockley Whins.

Class '56' diesels No. 56051 *Isle of Grain* and No. 56081 on the final day of South Dock Traincrew Depot and Fuelling Point on 9th April, 1994. The Prospect public house can be seen in the left background.

River Wear Commissioners 0-4-0ST No. 12 (Barclay, 1897) takes the last two wagons of creosote, destined for ICI at Billingham, from the Monsanto Chemical Works on 7th June, 1950, just before the Works closed. The Chemical Works, established as the Wear Fuel Works in 1871, were one of several industries around the Docks which were served by the River Wear Commissioners' (RWC) railway. Others included Bartram's Shipyard, the North East Marine Engine Works and several timber yards. For many years the RWC had about 10 locomotives for working in the Docks and on the construction and repair of piers.

DB Schenker No. 66001 at the press launch in Hudson Dock on 5th February, 2015 for the reopening of the railway link to the Docks after major refurbishment of the track which had been disused for several years. The line has subsequently been used for trains of scrap to Cardiff. The Port of Sunderland's locomotive shed is near the top of the photo with one of the two Ruston and Hornsby 0-4-0DEs; they were later given to the Bowes Railway.

The Old Main Line

The Durham Junction Railway opened in 1838 for freight and 1840 for passengers from Rainton Meadows, south of Fencehouses, to the Stanhope and Tyne Railway at Washington. It was designed as a through route from the South, but the connecting Newcastle and Darlington Junction Railway was only opened in 1844.

A shorter route for trains to Newcastle from Washington to Pelaw via Usworth was opened for goods in 1849 and passengers in 1850, but the railway lost its function as the East Coast Main when the new route via Durham was completed in 1872.

Passenger services were withdrawn from Usworth and Washington in 1963 and Penshaw and Leamside in 1964. The route remained open for freight and main line trains diverted because of engineering work on the Durham route until 1991, following the completion of the East Coast Main Line electrification.

No. D5148 and a brake tender (used to give extra weight for braking unfitted freight trains) heads a southbound goods train off the Victoria Bridge at Penshaw North on 26th August, 1964. The train is possibly for Durham Gilesgate. Under the signal box are the lines to Sunderland. At Cox Green Junction they will be joined by the Lambton lines on the right.

Class 'A1' 4-6-2 No. 60129 *Guy Mannering* passes Fencehouses station (also spelt as Fence Houses in the 19th century). It is heading a diverted Newcastle to London train in 1959. The station buildings on the left are the original Newcastle and Darlington Junction's structure designed by G.T. Andrews. To the right are the Lambton Railway's tracks with the pit head gear of Lambton D Colliery behind the houses and the Lambton Coke Works beyond.

Class 'A2/2' 4-6-2 No. 60502 *Earl Marischal* drifts through Penshaw with a diverted York to Glasgow express on Sunday 2nd July, 1959. Such Sunday diversions allowed engineering work to be carried out on the East Coast Main Line via Durham and were mentioned in the public timetable. The station buildings on the island platform of Penshaw station can be seen behind the last carriage of the train. The lines on the far left are those of the Lambton Railway.

A 'Q6' class 0-8-0 and brake van crosses the Victoria Bridge over the River Wear on 29th August, 1964.

Schoolboys write in the grime on 'V3' class 2-6-2T No. 67689 as it pauses at Washington with the evening train to Newcastle on 14th September, 1956. By this date there was only one timetabled train each way, used mainly by workers at Newalls Insulation and Chemical Works.

Newalls Insulation and Chemical Co.'s 0-4-0DH *Margaret* (English Electric Vulcan Works, 1966) at their Works on 28th October, 1970. The Works were originally owned by the Washington Chemical Company.

Class 'A4' 4-6-2 No. 60029 *Woodcock* heads south through Usworth with a diverted Edinburgh to King's Cross train on 23rd August, 1959. There was a branch to Usworth Colliery half a mile north of the station.

The Stanhope and Tyne and Hylton, Southwick and Monkwearmouth Railways

The Stanhope and Tyne Railway was opened from Stanhope to South Shields for freight in 1834 and for passengers in 1835. All services were suspended after the bankruptcy of the company in 1841 but resumed after the line was taken over by the Pontop and South Shields Railway.

On Wearside passenger services east of Washington ceased in 1853 when the Penshaw to Sunderland was opened and west of Washington in 1869. These sections closed to freight traffic in 1966, but the Washington to South Pelaw junction line was reinstated in 1974, finally closing in 1981.

The freight only Hylton, Southwick and Monkwearmouth Railway opened in 1876 from Southwick Junction on the Stanhope and Tyne to just North of Monkwearmouth station. It was linked by the Queen Alexandra Bridge to the Penshaw branch from 1909 to 1921. The line west of Hylton Colliery closed in 1925 and from Hylton Colliery to Southwick in 1975. In the 1980s Wearmouth Colliery became the western end of the line. The route closed completely at the same time as the colliery in 1993.

Class '9F' 2-10-0 No. 92065 approaches Biddick Lane level crossing, west of Washington, with an iron ore train from Tyne Dock to Consett on 18th July, 1966. The opening of the iron ore terminal at Tyne Dock in 1953 meant that iron ore was no longer imported through Sunderland South Docks. In the late 1860s there was a passenger station at Biddick Lane (*see map page 6*).

Class '25' No. D5182 propels a diesel brake tender on the Stanhope and Tyne line past Southwick Junction while returning from Washington to Tyne Dock on 3rd June, 1966. In the foreground is the course of the Hylton, Southwick and Monkwearmouth Railway (HSMR). The 8½ mile pipe carried salt water from a pumping station at the South Docks at Sunderland. Installed in 1940, the pipe ran beside the Penshaw branch to Millfield and then along the Queen Alexandra Bridge and the HSMR and the STR to the Chemical Works at Washington. Here magnesium was extracted from the sea water. The pipe can be seen in some of the photographs of the Penshaw branch

NCB 0-4-0ST No. 11 (Hudswell, Clarke, 1920) shunts at Hylton Colliery on 27th August, 1969. The colliery was built on the site of the Castletown Iron Works which was served by sidings from the HSMR.

'J27' class 0-6-0 No. 65788 heads a goods train between Hylton Colliery and Southwick on 23rd April, 1963 on the line used by BR. The right-hand track was used by NCB trains between Hylton and Wearmouth Collieries. The embankment on the right was for the line from Castletown Junction across the Queen Alexandra Bridge to Diamond Hall Junction on the Penshaw branch.

NCB 0-6-0DH No. 1 (North British Locomotive Co, 1955) shunts wagons at Wearmouth Colliery (in the right background) in June 1974. This was one of the first NCB diesel locomotives on Wearside and had previously worked on the Lambton and Hetton systems.

Network Rail's 1959-built class '31' No. 31105 leads the track recording train (with No. 31601 *Gauge '0' Guild 1956-2006* at the other end) at the single platform South Hylton station on 5th September, 2008. Because of the frequency of the Metro service the train was preparing to leave the station at 5.35 am before services started. The passage of a diesel locomotive on the line between South Hylton and Sunderland is extremely unusual, which local railway photographer Mark Grimes made sure he recorded.

On 2nd January, 1958 'A8' class 4-6-2 No. 69855 passes Ford Works with the siding to the paper works leading off to the right and to the quarry on the left. This train is the return working of a lunchtime service from Sunderland to Hylton on weekdays. On Wednesdays it ran to Penshaw, possibly for workers in Sunderland shops which closed in the afternoon on that day.

Ford Paper Works in 1883 showing the firm's locomotive and two of their chaldron wagons at the quay which was built on the Wear in 1880. The cost of the quay scheme was £900, including £572 0s. 10d. for the second-hand 0-4-0ST (Black, Hawthorn 1872). The Paper Works were connected to sidings on the higher Penshaw branch (behind chimney) by a rope-worked incline. The Paper Works steam, petrol and diesel locomotives were always confined to shunting at the foot of the incline. In the 1860s the first large scale use of esparto grass in paper making took place here. The Works, latterly owned by Wiggins Teape, closed in 1971.

Ford Quarry on 18th April, 1974 with wagons being loaded with crushed dolomite. The quarry, which was owned by Newalls Insulation and Chemical Company and was for several years the end of the Penshaw branch, ceased production in 1990. Narrow gauge diesel locomotives were at one time used at the bottom of the quarry.

NCB 0-6-2T No. 57 (Hawthorn, Leslie, 1934) coasts through Pallion station with a coal train for Lambton Staiths in 1963. Baskets from which pigeons had been released can be seen on the platform. The main station building on the left replaced those which lay on the opposite side of the line beyond the footbridge from which this photograph was taken. The original building had to be demolished when the line to Short's Shipyard was built about 1898.

NCB 0-6-2T No. 30 (Kitson, 1907) enters Pallion station with a brake van on its way from Lambton Staiths to Penshaw on 22nd April, 1963. This photograph shows the complexity of lines serving the various industries in the area. The track to the left of the signal box ran to Short's Shipyard, Steels Engineering and Coles Cranes, while that in the left background was for Deptford and Lambton Staiths.

'V2' class 2-6-2 No. 60828 approaches Pallion with a Sunderland to Manchester relief train travelling via Cox Green on 15th April, 1963. Jopling & Sons' Steel Works on the right were one of several forges and engineering works in Pallion.

Pallion Metro station on 15th April, 2018. The Metro was built on a new course, partly through the site of Doxford's Shipyard because of development on the trackbed and its use for the European Way Road. The Metro stations on the South Hylton line (apart from the sub-surface Park Lane) were built in a similar style with flat roofs, which is different from those elsewhere on the Metro, such as the Stadium of Light.

0-4-0CT *Roker* (Robert Stephenson and Hawthorns, 1940) working in Doxford's Shipyard on 3rd April, 1969. These locomotives, named after districts in Sunderland, were used as cranes as well as for shunting wagons.

Class '08' 0-6-0DE No. D3729 at Ogden's Lane on the Deptford branch on 25th March, 1970 propelling vans containing Pyrex glassware from Deptford to Pallion yard where they will be collected by a working to Tyne Yard. Shunter Alan Dent is waving the locomotive driven by Ernie Douglas over the level crossing. The brick base of the tall Ogden's Lane signal box, closed a month earlier, can be seen to the right. Lambton coal trains used the branch as far as Deptford Junction where they diverged on the line to the staiths.

J.D. Johnson's Deptford Landsale in the early 1960s. While side-door coal wagons predominated in most of Britain, wagons with bottom-doors which could be used at staiths for shipping were the rule in the North-East, hence the raised type of coal depot shown here. Rail traffic to Johnson's depot ceased in 1983.

Diamond Hall Junction signal box on 7th May 1966, the month the box closed. This controlled the junction for the line to Queen Alexandra Bridge opened in 1909 which did not produce the traffic the size of the box anticipated. The building to the right is on the site of the original section of James A. Jobling's Wear Glass Works, where all British-made domestic Pyrex was produced between 1922 and the closure of the works in 2007. As the demand for Pyrex increased, the factory expanded to the far side of the Deptford branch and its railway connection was moved twice to serve the new buildings.

Millfield station in the 1880s. This building was erected in 1864 to the design of Thomas Prosser, the NER's architect, who was also responsible for the main building at Hylton. The level crossing carried Hylton Road, although it was replaced by a bridge beyond the station by the time the line opened to passengers in 1853. In 1890 a new station was built on the west side of the bridge. The 1864 building survived as the station master's house. Its last use was as a public house before it was demolished so that the eastbound Metro platform could be built on its site.

Clayton No. D8594 heads a goods train through Millfield with vans containing Pyrex and paper to Tyne Yard on 26th May, 1970. The 1864 station building can be seen behind the brake van in front of the Hylton Road bridge on which the frontage of the 1890 station is situated. The main reason the passenger station was rebuilt was so that the westbound platform could be removed to allow expansion of the goods yard. By the time this photograph was taken, the raised coal landsale by the bridge could no longer be used and the coal depot had been moved to the goods yard. This meant that side-door wagons had to be used. The locomotive is passing the site of the junction for the line which led to Hylton Road and originally carried Lambton trains to the incline to the staiths.

Contractors lifting the rails near the Durham Road bridge in February 1985 so that the route could be converted into a foot and cycle path.

17 years after the previous photograph rails have been relaid and the University Metro station built on the site. Photographed on the Metro opening day on 31st March, 2002, it serves the City Campus of Sunderland University.

'B1' class 4-6-0 No. 61014 *Oribi* climbs out of Sunderland to Fawcett Street Junction with a special on Durham Miners' Gala Day on 21st July, 1962. The connection built in 1879 from Sunderland station to the higher Penshaw branch was steeply graded and some heavy passenger trains were banked by tank engines up this section. The line to the right is for South Dock. This is now the site of Park Lane Metro station.

Park Lane Metro station in April 2018. This was built as an interchange with the adjacent bus station. When opened it was reputed to be the second busiest bus station in the country (after Victoria in London), but this is now far from the case as many bus routes now avoid Park Lane on their journey through the City Centre. Things would have been very different if the Tyne and Wear integrated transport policy had not been ended by the deregulation of bus services.

Class 'G5' 0-4-4T No. 67253 along with Metro-Cammell dmus and parcels van in the Sunderland Central sidings photographed from Park Lane bridge on 11th September, 1958. On the right is Fawcett Street station, the passenger terminus of the Penshaw branch from 1853 to the opening of the new Sunderland station in 1879. The building survived until it was demolished to make way for the building of the Civic Centre car park.

'V3' class 2-6-2T No. 67653 propels a single van through Mowbray Park on the freight-only section of the Penshaw branch in March 1963. The ornamental cast-iron footbridge was built to connect the original section of the park to the Extension Park in 1866. It was restored as part of the refurbishment of the park and now crosses a footpath and flower beds.